BURT LANCASTER

a

singular

man

R O B Y N K A R N E Y

Trafalgar Square Publishing

For 'brother' Pete

ACKNOWLEDGEMENTS
Heartfelt thanks to Tom Vallance and Bernard Hrusa-Marlow in
London, and Marvin Eisenman in Los Angeles, for the trouble taken
in supplying me with copies of films, without which this book could
not have been written. As always, Clive Hirschhorn made his library
available, my researcher David Oppedisano worked beyond the call of
duty, and my long-standing colleague and friend Ronald Bergan gave
practical advice and moral support. Special thanks, too, to Christopher
Hahn in San Francisco; Howard Mandelbaum of Photofest in New
York; Juliet Brightmore, a picture researcher whose expertise is
further enhanced by her interest in the text; and my patient
copy-editor Richard Dawes.
    I will always be grateful to my agent, Tony Peake, for his
encouragement, and to my editor at Bloomsbury, Penny Phillips,
for her support and understanding.

First published in the United States of America in 1997 by
Trafalgar Square Publishing, North Pomfret, Vermont 05053

Printed in Hong Kong

Copyright © 1996 by Robyn Karney

The moral right of the author has been asserted

ISBN 1-57076-074-8

Library of Congress Catalog Card Number: 96-60857

10 9 8 7 6 5 4 3 2 1

Designed by Bradbury and Williams
Designer: Bob Burroughs

Picture research by Juliet Brightmore

PICTURE SOURCES
Joel Finler Collection, London.
Katz Pictures, London.
Katz Pictures/Snap-Photo.
Kobal Collection, London.
Photofest, New York, with acknowledgement to CBS TV, Lucas-
    Pritchard, NBC TV, Poletto, Rothschild.
Pictorial Press, London.
Range/Bettmann/Herb Scharfman.
Range/Bettmann/Springer.
Range/Bettmann/UPI.
Range Pictures/Everett.
Rex Features, London, with acknowledgement to Roberto Biciocchi,
    Dalmas, Globe Photos, Pierluigi, Sipa Press.
BFI Stills, Posters and Designs, London, with acknowledgement to
    American International Pictures, Artistes Associés/Ariane/Dear,
    Associated General, CBS TV, Cine-Neighbor/Selta, Columbia
    Pictures, Columbia/Filmways, Columbia/Horizon,
    Columbia/Norma, De Laurentiis/Lion's Gate, Enigma/Goldcrest,
    Hecht-Hill-Lancaster Productions, Hecht-Lancaster Productions,
    Lamitas/Samarkand, Lorimar-Bavaria/Geria, Metro-Goldwyn-
    Mayer, MGM/Hawn/Sylbert, NBC TV, Paramount Pictures
    Corporation, Paramount/Wallis, Rusconi/Gaumont, Scimitar
    Films, Seven Arts/Joel, Spartan/Mar Vista, Titanus/SNPC/SGC,
    Touchstone/Silver Screen/Bryna, United Artists Corporation,
    United Artists/Bryna, United Artists/James, United
    Artists/Scimitar, Universal/Gordon, Universal/Hellinger,
    Universal Pictures, Warner Brothers Inc., Warner Bros/Norma-FR.

Contents

Introduction

Burt Lancaster was the first, and the biggest, of the new crop of post-World War II stars and the last great survivor of Hollywood's golden era. In a career that began late and lasted some forty years, the former circus acrobat matured gracefully from handsome and famously smiling athletic hunk to dignified and authoritative elder statesman, bowing neither to time nor to changing fashion. In his earlier career, there was an almost disturbing disjunction between the grim, often doomed, tough-guy characters he played and his own extraordinary beauty. He lacked the uncomplicated directness of Gable, the ease of James Stewart or Henry Fonda, the sophisticated lightness of touch of Cary Grant or the saintly sincerity of Gregory Peck; and unlike all of those, his screen image constantly shifted as, uniquely for a major box-office star of the time, he tackled a very wide range of parts, constantly challenging himself beyond his natural abilities.

To some, Lancaster remains the embodiment of a doomed *film noir* victim, as in his debut film, *The Killers*; others harbour nostalgic memories of the swashbuckling action man, all teeth and smiles, as in *The Flame and the Arrow*. To the intelligentsia he is revered as the aristocratic Prince of Salina in *The Leopard* or the old lag trying a last trick in *Atlantic City*; while a new generation, thanks largely to television and video, has supplied a cult following for *The Swimmer* and is moved by *Birdman of Alcatraz*.

With seventy-seven feature films to his credit, he became rooted in the Hollywood landscape, always and inescapably just *there*. He lacked technical skill, and had neither the polish nor the suavity of a conventional leading man, while his distinctive voice, with its curious staccato delivery, frequently fell prey to mannerism and fuzzy diction. Yet actress Deborah Kerr, who made three films with him, identified one of the secrets of his success. 'Acting for the screen,' she said, 'is simply a matter of concentration, poured into the raising of an eyebrow or the dropping of an eyelid,' and named Lancaster (along with Cary Grant and Spencer Tracy) as one of the three actors who taught her this.

Conversely, no actor of his fame and standing gave as many indifferent or poor performances amid the fine work. Certainly the scope of his

LOU AND SALLY (LANCASTER, SUSAN SARANDON), TWO DREAMERS, IN LOUIS MALLE'S *ATLANTIC CITY* (1980).

ambitions was not always matched by the quality of his judgement, while his high intelligence and serious-minded commitment were sometimes abandoned, almost as a self-inflicted punishment for agreeing to appear in films that were unworthy of his oft-expressed ideals.

However, aside from his stupendous good looks, his formidable determination enabled him to outlast the studio system in whose demise, as the first major producer-star of the modern era, he played a significant role.

Lancaster was a complex and contradictory figure, an enigma in both his personal and his professional life. Something of a loner, and very much a committed family man, he was none the less an inveterate womanizer; a chain-smoking lover of good food and fine wines, he indulged these pleasures within the strictly disciplined regimen of a fitness fanatic. He spoke publicly for liberal democratic values, particularly on issues of race, and was known for his warmth, charm and generosity. But Lancaster's professional ego was monumental, his temper violent, and his convictions expressed with often brutal and cruelly insulting frankness.

Most importantly, in terms of his career, he transcended the limitations of his talent by the sheer weight and magnetism of his screen presence, which grew more imposing with each passing decade. He himself said, in a combined display of perspicacity and awesome ego, 'There is something about a man, his appearance or personality. You just want to see him again. An actor may have the skill but not the *presence*. It's so much more important in a film when your face is nine feet across in close-up. So people like myself might be schlepps as actors, but...'

That presence remains vivid in the memory of all who treasure his best work and cast a nostalgic glance back to the Hollywood of legend. As the American film historian David Thomson, echoing many another commentator, wrote, 'Brave, vigorous, handsome, and an actor of great range, Lancaster has never yielded in his immaculate splendor, proud to be a movie actor. And he has crept up on us, surviving, persisting, often in poor health. He is one of the great stars. Perhaps the last.'

Lancaster deserves to be remembered with respect and affection, a character of individuality and lasting interest, of whom the great Italian director of *The Leopard*, Luchino Visconti, said, 'The Prince himself was a very complex character – at times autocratic, rude, strong – at times romantic, good, understanding – and sometimes even stupid, and, above all, mysterious. Burt is all these things too. I sometimes think Burt is the most perfectly mysterious man I ever met in my life.'

Natural attributes

Like many a mythic screen hero before and since, Burt Lancaster was raised in humble circumstances and achieved fame and riches as much by accident as by design. He was helped considerably by the combination of a suitable temperament with a generous dose of good fortune. Reflecting on his debut in *The Killers* (1946), the respected *film noir* adapted from Hemingway, the actor himself acknowledged that 'a great case can be made here for luck... it was one of those instances of being the right actor in the right spot at the right time.'

Burton Stephen Lancaster was born on 2 November 1913, the third son (and fourth child) of James Lancaster, a $48-a-week clerk at the Madison Square Garden branch of the New York Post Office. Of Anglo-Irish stock, Jim enjoyed claiming direct descent from the Royal House of Lancaster – a claim neither proved nor disproved. But if the gift of an aristocratic lineage to his children was in some doubt, the blessing of good looks

The contradictions of character which would alternately enhance and bedevil his ambitions revealed themselves early on.

was not. Both he and his wife were exceptionally handsome, and their Nordically blond children were distinctive in a neighbourhood peopled by Italian and Jewish immigrants as well as Blacks.

The Lancasters lived on East 106th Street in a house which had been inherited by Burt's mother. It was divided into five flats (with a communal lavatory on each floor), which brought in a little extra income from rentals. The family, in common with the rest of the working-class neighbourhood, was poor, but not poverty-stricken, and Burt's recollections in later years were fond.

'Like our neighbours, we Lancasters just squeaked by, yet it was a

A CHARACTERISTIC PUBLICITY PICTURE OF BURT LANCASTER IN THE MID-FORTIES, EXUDING MACHO STRENGTH AND ALL-AMERICAN GOOD LOOKS.

rich life because there was a great deal of love and affection in our home. My mother was a strong-willed formidable character — a woman who insisted on honesty, truth and loyalty. My father was a gentle, kind, warm sort of a man. We lived well. I wore my brothers' hand-me-down clothes, true, but when you're young that just doesn't matter. So I was lucky. We had all the food we needed on the table…'

The 'formidable' Mrs Lancaster, who died when Burt was sixteen, was a major influence on the son who, for all the rough and tumble of the street life which taught him to fight, the hot temper which would take him half a lifetime to curb, and the streak of arrogance which never quite left him, grew up a man of honour, principled and loyal.

Undersized until his teens, he learned to use his fists early in defence against the dark-skinned kids on the block with whom he played and fought, and who nicknamed him 'Dutch'. He enjoyed the tough and raucous pursuits of this East Harlem childhood, and his reaction to the ethnic mix of his companions was a positive one, defining him in later years as one of Hollywood's genuine anti-racist liberal Democrats, a high-profile supporter of Martin Luther King and the Kennedys.

The contradictions of character which would alternately enhance and bedevil his ambitions, his judgements, and his personal and professional reputation, revealed themselves early on. At the schools he attended, PS 83 and De Witt Clinton High, he was an average pupil with no visible academic leanings. None the less, he was an avid reader who spent much time during his formative years devouring books in the public library; and a natural response to music developed into a lifelong passion, especially for opera, nurtured in the heavily Italian neighbourhood where

LANCASTER (CENTRE), AS THE ATHLETE HERO OF *JIM THORPE – ALL-AMERICAN* (1951), CROSSES THE FINISHING LINE IN A RACE AT THE COLLEGE WHERE HIS LEGENDARY GIFTS WERE DISCOVERED AND NURTURED.

acting was considered 'sissy' but sneaking into operatic performances (preferably without paying) was *de rigueur*. An ambition to be an opera singer led him to join the church choir, but he abandoned his vocal efforts when his voice broke. Attempts to learn the piano were also unsuccessful – the only one of his desired accomplishments that, according to him, he failed to master.

At the age of seven, a visit – to be much repeated – to the local movie theatre to see *The Mark of Zorro* kindled in the young Burt a hero-worship of Douglas Fairbanks and a passionate wish to emulate the exploits of the swashbuckling star. 'He'd go around the house jumping over everything in sight, trying to imitate Fairbanks' feats,' recalled Lancaster senior years later, adding that his son 'was a dreamer when he was a little kid. He could be off in his own world for hours and he wouldn't hear a thing you'd say to him. He grew up to be an essentially serious-minded guy, inclined to get intense about ideas and situations.'

But the focus of Burt Lancaster's youthful activities was the Union Settlement House on East 104th Street. This club-cum-sports centre provided opportunities to play basketball and do gymnastics, as well as making art, music and language courses available. The Settlement House also staged plays under the aegis of Richard Boleslawski's American Laboratory Theater. The Polish-born Boleslawski, who had worked at the Moscow Arts Theatre under Stanislavsky, and who would make a handful of movies in the thirties with stars such as Garbo and Dietrich, had instituted a scheme whereby, as part of their training, his students would direct amateur productions at settlement houses around Manhattan.

Thus, at an early age, Burt became accustomed to public performance. According to accounts, he proved adept, at least in the context of youthful amateur dramatics, and was offered an acting scholarship at the age of eleven. The offer was of no interest to the boy, whose thespian activities were not undertaken out of a burning desire to become an actor. 'I did it because I got "plus marks"; when you got enough plus marks, you would be sent off to summer camp. For a kid from East Harlem in the early 1920s, to go to summer camp was really something. You looked forward to it all year. That meant more than anything.'

A CURIOUSLY FEMININE AND BALLETIC BADMINTON POSE FOR YET ANOTHER IMAGINATIVE PUBLICITY PICTURE.

A SOMEWHAT
WISTFUL-LOOKING BURT,
PHOTOGRAPHED IN LESS
THAN IMPECCABLY
ELEGANT SUIT AND TIE.
HE LATER CAME TO BE
ACKNOWLEDGED,
OFF-SCREEN, AS ONE OF
THE WORST-DRESSED MEN
IN HOLLYWOOD.

It was during the years of Settlement House gymnastics and summer camps that Lancaster met Nick Cravat, a dark, wiry, pint-sized Italian-American who became his best friend. A boxing enthusiast, Cravat chalked up sixteen professional fights by the time he was eighteen and, according to Burt, 'could sink his fist into a lath-and-plaster wall'. Together, the two boys developed a taste for acrobatics and practised a hand-balancing act which turned into a more serious pursuit after Burt's graduation from De Witt Clinton High in 1929.

Now almost seventeen, Lancaster had shot up to six foot two of lithe, graceful muscle, and was blessed with the natural attributes of an athlete. In high school he had placed his instinctive aptitude for ball games at the service of basketball, and reached a level in the sport which earned him a scholarship to New York University. In the summer between high school graduation and the start of his freshman year, he and Nick Cravat encountered Charles 'Curly' Brent at the Settlement House. An Australian gymnast and ex-circus performer, Brent was working out on the horizontal bars in the gym when Lancaster and Cravat came by. Their fascination with Curly's routine resulted in the latter agreeing to teach them how to do bar swings, an activity that rapidly became obsessional. The Settlement House was persuaded to erect a second set of bars, while Burt rigged up yet a third set at home, where he worked tirelessly to perfect a routine.

In the autumn of 1929, Burton Lancaster commenced his courses at NYU, playing basketball, football and baseball, as well as participating in boxing, track events and gymnastics. His objective was to qualify as a physical education instructor and sports coach, but, although no academic, Lancaster wanted to learn more about the subjects that interested him. Regrettably, though, NYU was oversubscribed and understaffed and Burt found the lectures, delivered over a PA system with no questions allowed, tedious and unrewarding. Towards the end of 1931, in the depths of the Great Depression when work was hard to come by, he dropped out of college. 'I walked out of class one day and I never went back.'

Instead, it was off to the Settlement House and Curly Brent, where Burt and Nick Cravat worked up an acrobatic act and decided to take their chances on a life in the circus. In the spring of 1932 they scraped up ninety dollars for 'a fifth-hand jalopy' and, calling themselves 'Lang and Cravat', drove to Petersburg, Virginia, where the Kay Brothers Circus was setting up for a season. Despite a less than glittering audition, the boys were hired for a meagre three dollars a week plus board,

for which they were expected to help with the dozens of chores involved in staging a circus, from driving tent stakes into the ground to banner-carrying in the traditional street parades.

Six months on the road with the Kay Brothers was an education in the hard school of experience. They honed their existing skills, and expanded their repertoire by learning from the troupe's rather more seasoned gymnasts and acrobats. The ill-paid, back-breaking and nomadic existence of circus folk during the Depression supplied valuable lessons in the art of survival which indubitably contributed to Lancaster's thick skin in withstanding the later pressures of screen stardom. And the sense of ease that marks his performance in *Trapeze*, the big-top drama he made in 1956, must be attributed in some part to the actor's art imitating his life.

From their apprenticeship with the Kay Brothers, the duo went on to a succession of engagements with small circuses, as well as performing at carnivals and in vaudeville — anywhere, in fact, that would hire them and enable them to eat — and they added a perch-pole routine to their act that would resurface in *The Flame and the Arrow* in 1950. In 1935 Burt met and fell in love with June Ernst, a circus aerialist who, according to him, was the only woman in the USA who could perform horizontal tricks on the bar. Clearly dazzled by this achievement, he married her,

His extraordinary good looks were insufficient — studios, so they claimed, were looking for experienced actors.

but the relationship survived for barely a year. The only comment Lancaster ever made about the brief liaison was that 'it didn't work out. We never had any fights. We just got tired of each other.' The parting and subsequent divorce were amicable enough: subsequently, Lang and Cravat, for a brief spell, even performed an act with Burt's erstwhile mother-in-law, a trapeze artist.

The vicissitudes of circus life continued. The high point was a $300-a-week stint with the famous Ringling Brothers, then it was back to the nightclub circuit for a mere twentieth of that sum. In the mid-thirties Burt decided to take time out and look again at the 'sissy' pursuit of his youth, acting.

Returning to New York, he joined the Federal Theater Project, a branch of Franklin D. Roosevelt's Work Projects Administration, which the President had established as part of the New Deal for Depression-hit Americans. Lancaster studied acting, taught by professionals who had trained with the same Richard Boleslawski whose students had directed

at the Union Street Settlement House.

It was a rich time for the New York theatre, and a culture-hungry Burt relished a diet of the best that Manhattan had to offer. As he remembered it, 'That was the place and that was the time. I can remember seeing Lillian Hellman's *The Children's Hour* in 1935... A year later I saw John Gielgud's Hamlet. It was the first Shakespeare I'd ever seen... Orson Welles was with the Federal Theater, there was the Group, the Civic Repertory and Boleslawski's American Lab.'

But despite his adult enthusiasm for the drama, he still felt more comfortable in the air than on the ground. He rejoined Cravat and started the cycle of hand-to-mouth work all over again. During an engagement in Los Angeles he made the rounds of movie casting offices, more out of curiosity and restlessness than clear ambition, but his extra-ordinary good looks were insufficient — studios, so they claimed, were looking for experienced actors.

LITTLE AND LARGE: BURT SHOULDER-HOISTS HIS BUDDY AND PARTNER, PINT-SIZED NICK CRAVAT.

A solid seven years of struggle were beginning to take their toll and Lancaster, albeit lacking a clear sense of direction for his future, was aware that he was growing frustrated and dissatisfied with a life that appeared to offer little prospect of security or advancement. By 1939 he was seriously looking at quitting the circus, when he tore open the fore-finger of his right hand during a rehearsal in St Louis. It became too badly infected to continue work, and he left the show with 'one suit — the one on my back — and twenty bucks in my kick.' He made for Chicago, where circus friends, the Smiletas, were able to put him up. Nick found a new partner, female this time, whom he later married.

From his refuge with the Smiletas, Lancaster, ill qualified for a profes-sion, took a job at Marshall Fields, Chicago's grand department store. He began in the ladies' lingerie department, was moved to men's haber-dashery, and fetched up in furniture. After the peripatetic life of the

circus, the circumscribed existence of a store salesman sat ill
with him. After a few months he
attempted to alleviate his bore-
dom by kidding the customers
with antics that included walking
down the aisles on his hands. He
left the store in favour of a refrig-
eration company that supplied
Chicago's meat-packing plants,
finding it more agreeable to be on
the move from plant to plant,
where he made the daily tempera-
ture adjustment to the coolers.

The outlook improved when he
applied for, and got, a position
with the New York-based
Community Concert Bureau, an
arm of CBS. The Bureau sold and
promoted concerts round the
country, via civic organizations,
and hired Burt as a $6,000-a-year
salesman to travel the country. In
a 1948 interview with the *Saturday
Evening Post* he described the job in
characteristically colourful New Yorkese: 'I was supposed to fix it so
Junior Leaguers could sit in concert halls scratching themselves in a
genteel and ladylike manner while they listened to Lawrence Tibbett or
some other canary popping off onstage. The trick was to sell them a
package deal...'

But in July 1942, as he was about to commence work, Burt received
his call-up papers. To occupy the time before his induction into the
army, he worked as a singing waiter in a downmarket New Jersey nightclub, then presented himself at Fort Riley, Kansas, for training. Private
Lancaster was assigned to the Special Services Division of the Fifth
Army, where, thanks to his circus background, he was attached to the
entertainment unit. The Fifth Army took him to North Africa, Sicily,
Austria and Italy, and kept him busy writing sketches, directing shows,
and occasionally appearing in them. Opinionated and independent-
minded, he argued with his superiors, notably with the lieutenant in

charge of a revue called *Stars and Gripes*, thus ensuring that his periodic promotions to the rank of sergeant were short-lived.

On balance, Burt Lancaster enjoyed his time in uniform, happily admitting, 'I never had one heroic moment.' He did, however, acquire an ease and familiarity with military conduct and bearing that would serve him well in his acting career, together with a love of Italy, where he would later buy a second home. He also met an attractive young war widow named Norma Anderson, who was performing in a touring show with the USO for the soldiers in Italy.

By the summer of 1945 he was home in New York, still in uniform and awaiting demob. Norma Anderson, back at her pre-war job with RCA radio producer Ray Knight, promised him an introduction to her boss who, she hoped, might help to find Burt a peacetime job. It was in the Rockefeller Center elevator that the legendary luck began smiling on Lancaster. He was on his way up to Norma's office to collect her for lunch when he was disconcerted by the stare of a fellow passenger. The man followed Lancaster out of the elevator and asked whether he was an actor, receiving the reply, 'Yes, I'm a dumb actor.'

As Burt recalled, 'I was kidding, referring to an expression – dumb actor – that's used in the circus when you do an act and then don't talk. Acrobats are all called "dumb actors".'

His perfect ease in military uniform was a lasting legacy of the war years, as seen in this photograph taken on the set of *From Here to Eternity* (1953).

The man was Jack Mahlor, an associate of Broadway producer Irving Jacobs who was casting a new play, *A Sound of Hunting*, about a group of GIs caught in the ravages of Monte Cassino during the hostilities which had only so recently ended. Lancaster's physical presence struck Mahlor as perfect for the lead role of Sergeant Mooney, and he was invited to read for it.

On 21 November 1945, after a two-week try-out in Philadelphia, *A Sound of Hunting* opened at the Lyceum Theatre, New York, with Burton Lancaster, aged thirty-two years and nineteen days, co-starring with a cast that included the well-known character actor Sam Levene. Despite excellent notices, war-weary audiences stayed away in their droves, and the production folded after twenty-three performances. (The play was filmed eight years later by Columbia as *Eight Iron Men*, with Lee Marvin in the Lancaster role.)

BURT ON STAGE WITH FRIEND AND CO-STAR SAM LEVENE IN *A SOUND OF HUNTING* AT THE LYCEUM THEATRE, NEW YORK, IN NOVEMBER 1945.

The three-week run, however, proved enough to win Burt a Theatre World award and good reviews (the *New York Journal-American* thought that 'Burton Lancaster, as Mooney, is the non-com every private prays for'), while his commanding physical presence, exceptional good looks, and sincerity of performance were noted by the Hollywood talent scouts who regularly trawled the New York theatres in search of fresh talent.

Within weeks of the play's closure, Lancaster had an agent, a first-class ticket to Los Angeles, and a provisional film contract subject to a screen test.

Brute force

The skills were uncertain and the image ambiguous, but the rise was meteoric. With *A Sound of Hunting* attracting Hollywood offers, Burt's fellow actor Sam Levene advised him to find an agent and introduced him to Harold Hecht. The son of a New York iron merchant, Hecht was six years older than Lancaster, with a show-business provenance that stretched back some two decades. He had begun his career at the American Laboratory Theater with Richard Boleslawski when he was sixteen, and had assisted the Polish director on several stage productions as well as acting in a number of Broadway plays. He then switched to dance, performing most notably with Martha Graham's company before going during the early thirties to Hollywood, where he worked as dance director on such films as the Marx Brothers' *Horse Feathers* and Mae West's *She Done Him Wrong*. He returned to the straight theatre in 1934, joining the Federal Theater Project, then became a Hollywood literary agent. Now, back from war service, he was attempting to expand his agency to include actors and directors.

> 'Here we were, a couple of bums
>
> without a quarter between us,
>
> discussing producing our
>
> own pictures.'

The first meeting between Lancaster and Hecht, held over dinner in New York, was a success. Both were ambitious and outspoken, and their ambitions appeared to coincide with miraculous synchronicity. In a well-documented exchange between them, Hecht said, 'I know everybody, but I have few clients. If you sign with me you'd be important to me. I'd work harder for you, because I want to eat and I'd have to keep you working.'

Lancaster found Hecht's attitude impressive, and their evident rapport was cemented later in the evening when Hecht confided that his

AS SHERIFF TOM HANSON
IN THE UNDISTINGUISHED
DESERT FURY, HIS FIRST
FILM IN COLOUR.

real aspiration lay in becoming a film producer. Years later, according to an interview Burt gave Hedda Hopper, Hecht's statement struck a chord in the fledgeling actor. 'That was what I wanted to do. Suddenly we began laughing. Here we were, a couple of bums without a quarter between us, discussing producing our own pictures. Hecht laughed and said, "You never can tell. Maybe in five years we can make it." '

Meanwhile there was the practical matter of sifting through several Hollywood proposals. The most advantageous contract was offered by Hal B. Wallis, who had seen *A Sound of Hunting* and had presented himself in Burt's dressing-room after the show. According to Wallis, 'Looking at Burt's huge shoulders and capable hands, I knew women would be delighted with him. I... complimented him on his performance and offered him a job in our stock company. Burt was cool and quite unimpressed, suggested that I see his agent and closed his dressing-room door.' This characteristic refusal on Lancaster's part to be impressed by status would prove a key component in getting his own way over the years.

Chicago-born Hal Wallis was a production mogul of the old school, who had risen from publicity department assistant at Warner Bros. in 1923 to executive in charge of production until 1944, presiding over the studio's golden years, which saw a string of hits from *Little Caesar* (1930) to *Casablanca* (1943).

At the time of his approach to Lancaster, the commercially astute producer had formed Hal Wallis Productions with an office at Paramount, and was putting together a small stock company of young unknown contract players whom he intended to build into stars. In addition to blonde, husky-voiced Lizabeth Scott, a sort of cut-price Lauren Bacall, and the excellent Broadway actor Wendell Corey, he had signed a young actor named Kirk Douglas, whose debut film, *The Strange Love of Martha Ivers*, starring Barbara Stanwyck, would be released in 1946.

Wallis' offer to Lancaster was contingent upon the actor's making a successful screen test, in which case he would be given a contract, initially renewable over a total period of seven years, and required to make two pictures per year. What made the deal more attractive than similar offers was the inclusion of a clause that would allow Lancaster to make a third picture in any one year for any outside company of his choosing.

BEFORE HOLLYWOOD'S COSMETIC DENTISTS CLOSED THE RATHER CHARMING GAPS IN THE FAMOUSLY FLASHING TEETH!

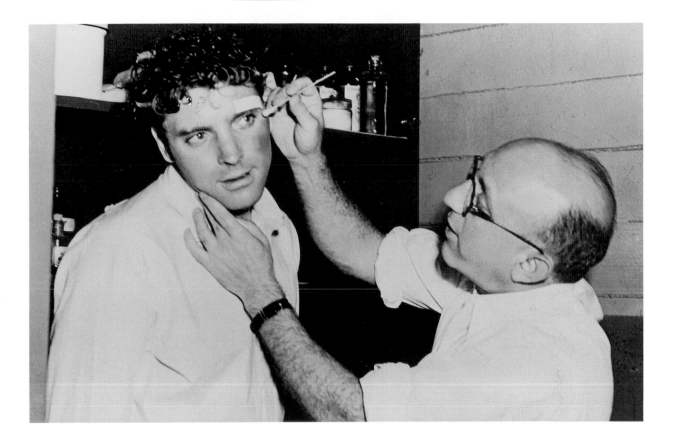

On this basis, Hecht negotiated a modest $100-a-week salary for the period of screen-test preparation, a flat fee of $10,000 should the test prove acceptable, and a weekly pay cheque of $1,250 on commencement of work.

In January 1946, with thirty dollars to his name, Lancaster arrived in Los Angeles and was sent to read for Wallis staff director Byron Haskin. The reading proved a declaration of Burt's serious intent: he rearranged the office furniture to represent the front-line trench in *A Sound of Hunting* and launched into an uninhibited performance of a blood-and-guts scene from the play. This went down well, and the test went ahead.

Unbeknown to Burt, the test material was from a script that Wallis intended as the actor's first film under the new contract. It would emerge in the autumn as *Desert Fury*, but shooting was not scheduled for some months, leaving a frustrated Burt kicking his heels. He decided to return to New York and the charms of Norma Anderson, when the famous Lancaster luck intervened. The noted journalist, critic, screenwriter, Broadway producer and associate film producer Mark Hellinger – for whom a Broadway theatre was later named – had recently set up his own film company, operating out of Universal's studios, and had acquired the rights to Ernest Hemingway's short story *The Killers* for his first independent venture. Hellinger was having trouble casting the key role of Ole Andreson, known as 'The Swede', a dumb boxer who is drawn into the criminal underworld and is destroyed by it, both metaphorically and – by the killers of the title – literally.

DIRECTOR ROBERT SIODMAK PERSONALLY TOUCHES UP THE ROOKIE MOVIE ACTOR'S FIGHT INJURY MAKE-UP FOR *THE KILLERS*, LANCASTER'S DEBUT FILM AND AN INSTANT SUCCESS.

Hellinger's first choice was Warner Bros. actor Wayne Morris, who had made a name as *Kid Galahad* before the war, but Warners wanted more money for the loan-out than was available. Lancaster, a self-proclaimed Hemingway aficionado, heard of Hellinger's difficulties and persuaded Wallis employee Marty Juroc to sneak a copy of the *Desert Fury* screen test to the producer. This led to a meeting between Hellinger and Burt, who turned the well-known actor's trick of behaving like the character he was hoping to play.

Hellinger recalled, 'This guy was big, really big. His hair was tousled. No tie... But there was something about him. All the time I was talking to him, that smart guy was playing the dumb Swede for me. The Swede I had in mind was big, dumb, awkward and fumbling. The day I met him Lancaster was all four. When you get to know him you realize he's anything but the last three.'

Asked by Hellinger what he thought of the Anthony Veiller screenplay, Burt dropped the pretence and replied, 'Well, the first sixteen pages are pure Hemingway verbatim, and after that you have a rather interesting whodunnit film, but nothing comparable to Hemingway. He said, "Well, you're not really a dumb Swede after all," and I said I didn't think I was.'

Perhaps the richest, and certainly the most complex, genre in American cinema is that of *film noir*. The *noir* form, with its moodily-lit world whose murky exterior reality reflects interior disturbance, emerged during the early forties, reaching one of its highest peaks of achievement with Billy Wilder's *Double Indemnity* in 1944.

The thirty-two-year-old newcomer worked hard, doing what was asked of him and displaying appropriate humility.

Robert Siodmak, one of the foremost exponents of *film noir*, had begun his career, alongside Wilder, Fritz Lang and Fred Zinnemann, in his native Germany. The rise of Hitler forced him, along with his several Jewish colleagues, into exile in 1933. His feeling for the techniques of German Expressionism had already distinguished two of his Hollywood films, *The Phantom Lady* (1944) and *The Spiral Staircase* (1945), and his talent for evoking claustrophobic tension was ideally suited to *The Killers*.

The film's much-praised opening sequences are a reasonably faithful realization of the Hemingway original. Two hired guns arrive at a small-town diner in the early evening, looking for The Swede. Using threats against the diner's staff, they get his address and leave. Nick Adams, a

THE STAR OF *THE KILLERS*
RELAXES BETWEEN TAKES
WITH VIRGINIA CHRISTINE
(RIGHT), WHO PLAYED THE
GIRL HE JILTS, AND AVA
GARDNER, WITH WHOM AN
OFF-SCREEN ROMANCE
WAS RUMOURED.

young man present at the scene, rushes to warn The Swede, whom he finds lying on his boarding-house bed in the gloom. In their brief exchange, it is clear that the man has both expected and resigned himself to his impending fate. Nick leaves, the thugs arrive, and their target is hit with a fusillade of shots.

From this point on, Hemingway is left behind and the screenwriter takes over to unravel, in flashback, the events that led Ole Andreson to degenerate from prizefighter to criminal, to victim double-crossed by an irresistible but poisonous woman. The latter was played by Ava Gardner, herself *en route* to major stardom and recognition as one of the world's most beautiful women – a journey helped considerably by the success of *The Killers*. Edmond O'Brien was the investigator on the trail of The Swede's past, and Burt's friend Sam Levene the cop who helps him.

Most reports of the eight-week shoot record that the thirty-two-year-old newcomer behaved as befits a novice, working hard, doing what was asked of him and displaying appropriate humility. He showed a degree of uncertainty that would prove short-lived in his career, apologizing profusely for necessitating multiple retakes of one particular scene.

However, in her autobiography, Ava Gardner hints that early signs of Burt's soon-to-be dictatorial manner with directors could be detected. 'Burt had all the confidence in the world. He'd never been in a movie before, but he seemed competent enough to take the whole thing over, and if Robert [Siodmak] hadn't been such a strong director, he might have.' She also reflected that 'One thing I especially liked about filming *The Killers* was that Burt and Eddie and the rest of us were in the early stages of our careers, fresh kids enjoying life.' It would appear, too, that Ava and Burt enjoyed each other off-screen.

Released in New York on 28 August 1946, *The Killers* garnered reviews that ranged from respectable to enthusiastic and was a box-office success. Its unknown star, given top billing, was acknowledged as 'a likeable fall guy in a most promising debut' by the *Herald Tribune*, while the show-business bible, *Variety*, credited him with having done a 'strong job'. In Britain, Harris Deans of the now-defunct *Sunday Dispatch* had the prescient 'feeling that we're going to see more of Burt Lancaster'.

Lancaster's own comment was that 'I could be very simple in the part. There was no need to be highly ostentatious or theatrical. For a new actor this is much easier than something histrionic.' This perceptive assessment is all the more interesting in the light of certain later

performances in which Lancaster's ostentatious histrionics play havoc with the material. In his superb book on *film noir*, *The Dark Side of the Screen*, Foster Hirsch suggests that Burt was 'never more interesting than in his early *noir* roles'. He identifies 'dark undertones lurking between Lancaster's healthy grin' and remarks that 'the tangled combination in Lancaster's early persona of beauty and perversity makes a striking dramatic impact'. These are acute observations, penetrating the nerve-centre of the actor's strengths.

Burt Lancaster was a creature of great physical beauty, graceful and god-like – the all-American athlete with the Colgate smile – yet able to suggest vulnerability beneath the macho surface. Thanks to his serendipitous debut, his early screen 'heroes' were characterized by knuckle-headed decency at odds with otherwise criminal behaviour. Unlike his contemporaries Kirk Douglas and Robert Mitchum, tough guys to the last, Burt occupied the doomed territory of the naively honourable patsy. He would rapidly come to be categorized as a *noir* exponent, only to confuse the expectations of his public in a career which constantly changed direction.

Capitalizing on the success of their first joint outing, Hellinger signed Burt for two more films, *Brute Force*, and another yet to be decided. Meanwhile, Hal Wallis, realizing he had a potentially bigger star under contract than even he had anticipated, ordered expansionary rewrites to Burt's secondary role in *Desert Fury*, and allowed the actor to proceed with *Brute Force* in the interim.

After that film was completed, the cameras were finally turned on

Desert Fury. As the straightforwardly moral law officer in a small Arizona town who rescues the object of his affections from the dangerous clutches of a murderous professional gambler, Burt had little to do other than look strong, handsome and reliable. Despite Wallis' much-trumpeted rewrites, the role of Sheriff Tom Hanson remained stubbornly secondary and uninteresting, with the limelight focused on John Hodiak as the villain, fellow contract players Lizabeth Scott and Wendell Corey

BELOW LEFT: IRON JAW, IRON FIST. A STRONG MOMENT FOR BURT'S OTHERWISE BLAND HERO IN *DESERT FURY* AS HE THREATENS VILLAIN JOHN HODIAK, HIS RIVAL FOR THE AFFECTIONS OF LIZABETH SCOTT IN WHOM, RIGHT, HE CONFIDES HIS HOPES AND DREAMS.

(excellent in his first film), and Mary Astor — who had graced better scripts than this in her heyday — hauled in to play Scott's tough, gambling saloon-owner mother. A dreary farrago in lurid Technicolor, *Desert Fury* came and went, leaving Lancaster to observe, 'If I'd done it first, it's impossible to say how long it would have been before I'd have been given anything that captured the public's fancy.'

With his career set to prosper, Burt married Norma Anderson in Yuma, Arizona on 28 December 1946. The couple, with Norma's small son from her first marriage, took a house at Malibu, but within a year they moved to a Bel Air mansion, opulent symbol of stardom and money. The move was necessitated by the need to accommodate Burt's widowed father, his older brother Jim, now retired from the police force, and the first of his own children, William, born on 17 November 1947. If the choice of house and neighbourhood and, indeed, the additions to it over the years — including the building of a baseball diamond in the grounds and a valuable art collection — indicated a taste for the high life, it was misleading. Lancaster remained a family man and something of a loner, pursuing his enthusiasm for books and music. He took

HAPPY TIMES: BURT AND HIS WIFE, THE FORMER NORMA ANDERSON.

Caged men, cut off from their women by a wall of stone and steel..!

MARK HELLINGER TELLS IT THE "KILLERS" WAY

up golf and became a keen bridge player, but he made few personal friends and avoided becoming a fixture on the nightclub, party and gossip circuit.

Wallis had had the perspicacity to hold back the release of *Desert Fury*, in which Burt was only third-billed, until the autumn of 1947, allowing *Brute Force* to open first. This ensured a second consecutive success for a top-billed Burt in a strong, violent prison drama which remains highly regarded in the annals of the genre. The screenplay was written by Richard Brooks, later to become a successful director, who would cross professional paths again with Lancaster to their mutual Oscar-winning advantage. The plot of the film concerns plans for a prison break-out, masterminded by Joe Collins (Lancaster) who, with his cell mates, has been driven to desperation by the corrupting brutality with which the place is run by a sadistic, Wagner-loving chief officer (Hume Cronyn) and an ineffectual governor blind to the situation. The weakness of the script lies in characterizing the escapees as a bunch of nice guys, each and every one of whom has landed up behind bars because of misguided efforts to please a woman.

THE 'COME-ON' POSTER FOR *BRUTE FORCE* BELIED THE FILM'S RAW POWER AND THE PERIPHERAL ROLES OF THE WOMEN.

These events are shown in flashback, and we learn that Burt's crime was committed to help his adored wife, an invalid. But these structural lapses, introduced to raise the movie's marquee value with the presence of attractive women, do not ultimately detract from the raw power of the film and, since the convict heroes all meet horrible deaths, Hollywood was able to uphold its moral stance while transmitting its anti-violence message. The film was directed by Jules Dassin, who handled the material in a skilful and uncompromisingly chilling manner. (After his next film, Dassin was named as a Communist during the McCarthy hearings and was forced into exile.)

Burt acknowledged Dassin as a fine director, but during filming he displayed his penchant for interference for the first time. This tendency to know better than the director would grow pronounced, often causing tension and dissension, despite the actor's avowed respect for talented and professional colleagues. The character of Joe Collins, divorced from the context of the action, is, in reality, fairly one-dimensional and unchallenging, but it is in marked contrast to that of The Swede. Joe is strong, focused and courageous and meets his end with honour. It was also the first role that exposed one of Lancaster's primary gifts — the ability to convey suppressed rage simmering beneath a silent and stoical surface. Bosley Crowther of the *New York Times*, unimpressed by Burt's performance in *The Killers*, remained lukewarm about both star and film, confining his comments to 'big-framed expressionless Burt Lancaster gives the chief convict a heroic mold'; but the *Herald Tribune* considered his performance 'brooding' and 'effective'.

With almost two years as a full-time Hollywood actor behind him, and an extraordinary degree of status considering the relative paucity of his output, Lancaster had grown confident, indeed arrogant, in his opinions. He held the literate Hellinger in esteem, but was almost contemptuous of Wallis, of whom he said, 'His name is on *Casablanca* and some others, but that was because he was an executive producer at Warner Brothers. He had nothing to do with the pictures, nothing to speak of, nothing creative. When he became his own producer, he set out to make money.' Burt had by now developed a serious and admirable conviction that the secret of a quality film lay in the quality of the script. It was a line he was to pursue vigorously and one that would pay several dividends, particularly in his capacity as a producer. But it also highlighted his hard-nosed commercial acumen which led him to justify the acceptance of numerous acting assignments in films that fell far short of his professed standards.

Lancaster possessed a notoriously violent temper, but on the screen he was capable of much gentleness and sensitivity.

He had no say in the choice of material for his next film, since it was under his Wallis contract. *I Walk Alone*, directed by Byron Haskin, also featured the other core members of the Wallis stable, Lizabeth Scott, Wendell Corey and, notably, Kirk Douglas. The rasping tough guy with the cleft chin had made an impact in *The Strange Love of Martha Ivers* the previous year and was well on the way to star status that would equal, and in some regards surpass, Lancaster's own. The two men were not dissimilar: both self-made, they were opinionated, egocentric and ambitious. Their differences, though were marked. In life, Lancaster

FRAMED BY NOLL TURNER (KIRK DOUGLAS) AND UNDER THREAT, FRANKIE MADISON (LANCASTER) IS HELPED BY NIGHTCLUB SINGER KAY (LIZABETH SCOTT), NOLL'S DISILLUSIONED GIRLFRIEND, IN *I WALK ALONE*.

possessed a notoriously violent temper, but on the screen he was capable of much gentleness and sensitivity, qualities which rarely surfaced in Douglas' screen persona. He was also by far the handsomer and more glamorous of the two, but Douglas was, from the beginning, the confident, uninhibited actor.

When one looks at their collaborative films, it is interesting to see that their roles are very seldom interchangeable. This is certainly so with *I Walk Alone*, which marked the first of six films together, and the start of a lifelong friendship composed of rivalry and respectful affection in equal measure.

In the movie, Frankie Madison (Lancaster) who took the rap for his partner Noll Turner (Douglas) on a rum-running charge during Prohibition, is released from jail and comes to collect his share of the money from his buddy. Now the owner of a fashionable Manhattan nightclub, and involved in organized crime, Noll dupes, betrays, and finally attempts to kill Frankie, who, helped by Kay (Scott), the club's singer and Noll's badly treated girlfriend, delivers Turner into the arms of the cops. Lancaster's persona fitted the role like a glove, and this time he was allowed to be positive – a survivor who gets the girl, beats the baddie and, by his implied conversion to respectability, emerges a hero despite his criminal history. The film was only reasonably well received, though Douglas got raves, but, seen today, it is an entertaining crime melodrama, hovering very close to the edges of the *film noir* formula, and Frankie Madison was lumped in with Burt's previous *noir* protagonists, contributing to a growing image that would require some effort to change.

The first opportunity to depart from type came with a loan-out to producer Chester Erskine at Universal to appear in *All My Sons*. Arthur Miller's play had been directed by Elia Kazan on Broadway, where it had completed a respectable run and won the Drama Critics Circle Award in 1947. A probing, serious – and, in the aftermath of World War II, timely – examination of personal ethics, it was powerful drama but hardly the stuff of movie box office. Putting his money where his mouth was, Burt was willing, along with the rest of the cast, to take a substantial salary cut in the interests of making a serious film of literary quality, and one that would provide an opportunity to broaden his hitherto limited range

of characters. His enthusiasm was not shared by Wallis, who could not profit from the deal, but Burt's persistence forced the producer to acquiesce.

The central role of Joe Keller was to be played by the formidable Edward G. Robinson. Keller is an industrialist who has been tried and acquitted for selling defective aeroplane parts to the US government, thus causing the deaths of wartime flyers – one of whom was his own son, Larry. Burt played the other son, Chris. The apex of the many conflicts, fears and passions in the play is Chris' discovery that his father is indeed guilty of the crime (and therefore Larry's death) and that he knowingly shifted the blame on to his former partner, now languishing in jail. Matters are further complicated because the partner's daughter is the girl Chris wants to marry.

Directed by Irving Reis, the film remains true to the framework and focus of the play while opening it out and attempting to soften its didacticism. Though never a popular commercial success, it is a gripping

RIGHT: AS THE WEAK AND TORMENTED HENRY STEVENSON PUSHED INTO MURDER IN *SORRY, WRONG NUMBER*.

LOUISA HORTON (AS THE GIRL CHRIS KELLER LOVES), EDWARD G. ROBINSON, MADY CHRISTIANS AND LANCASTER IN *ALL MY SONS*.

piece with a powerhouse performance from Robinson and a respectable one from Lancaster, making his first foray into a conventional collar-and-tie character. He is sincere, attractive and, in the key confrontation with his father, passionately eloquent, but he lacks ease and bite, betraying his shortage of formal training or wide acting experience.

The actor had a mixed critical reception, being accused by *Time and Tide* of an 'apparent inability to express anything other than dumb toughness or dumb devotion', but the British *Daily Mail*'s critic felt it was 'the first time I have seen Mr Lancaster act with more than his biceps and his jaw'. The *Herald Tribune* paid him the compliment of giving him an equal share in the praise of his rather more illustrious co-stars. In his autobiography, Edward G. Robinson noted his commitment and wrote that the actor had demonstrated the 'animal vitality and suppressed volcano inside that inevitably made him a star'.

And indeed that stardom did seem to be inevitable. Despite his lack of polish and the fact that, in reality, he had enjoyed only two popular successes out of five films, he was blessed with the requisite chemistry for a screen star. *All My Sons* was released in March 1948, and in May Burt had his first experience of radio, giving a live broadcast of *I Walk Alone* (with Lizabeth Scott and Kirk Douglas) for Lux Radio Theatre; then, in November, he and Robinson repeated their roles for NBC's radio version of *All My Sons*.

If *All My Sons* had given the actor a taste of a different dramatic milieu, it did little to break the mould in which he was becoming set and which would show itself in one form or another in three

consecutive parts. The first of these took dogged determination to persuade a reluctant Wallis to allow him to play. Lucille Fletcher's radio play *Sorry, Wrong Number* had enjoyed phenomenal success on the 'Suspense' hour in 1943, and had since been broadcast eight times in five years. It had been a personal triumph for the distinguished actress Agnes Moorehead, in what was virtually a solo piece, as a wealthy, bedridden woman who, left alone in her apartment, tries to call her husband and overhears two men plotting a murder to take place a few hours later. Gradually, it becomes apparent that she herself is the victim. She is not a young woman, and both her husband and any references to their relationship are entirely absent from the script.

Using this central premise, the film focuses at first on the young, glamorous Leona, a wealthy, domineering and neurotic heiress, who marries Henry Stevenson, a handsome, ambitious but weak young man from the wrong side of the tracks. The plot moves from there to arrive at the core of the radio play. Wallis felt that Moorehead was not enough of a box-office name to repeat her *tour de force* on screen, and had cast the magnificent Barbara Stanwyck as Leona Stevenson, but the part of Henry was proving more difficult to fill.

Despite the fact that the spotlight would indubitably remain on the actress, Lancaster desperately wanted the husband's role. Wallis regarded him as far too strong and heroic a figure to fill the shoes of a henpecked moral weakling, but Burt pressed his case, arguing that 'a strong-looking boy on the threshold of life allows a woman to buy him and then suffers for it, and all of his character has been drained out of him. And at the beginning of the film, they'll believe I'm strong, and the contrast will make for real excitement.'

It was a shrewd appraisal, and with Burt's marquee value estimated at a minimum of $1 million, the producer discussed the idea with director Anatole Litvak and Lancaster got his way. Released in September 1948, *Sorry, Wrong Number* is a claustrophobic, nail-biting *noir* thriller with an original twist in having a female protagonist. Stanwyck earned one of her several Oscar nominations for her performance, the picture grossed a great deal of money, and Lancaster emerged with his reputation enhanced. In the opinion of *Look* magazine, 'Burt Lancaster continues his steady advance from muscle-man to accomplished actor,' and the *Herald Tribune*'s Howard Barnes found him 'grimly persuasive', but Bosley Crowther, who had yet to say a good word for the actor, stood his ground in the *New York Times*, calling Lancaster's performance 'painfully obtuse'.

LEFT: WITH JOAN
FONTAINE IN *KISS THE
BLOOD OFF MY HANDS,*
THE FIRST FILM PRODUCED
BY HAROLD HECHT AND
BURT FOR THEIR OWN
COMPANY, HECHT-NORMA.
RIGHT: LURKING IN THE
SHADOWS OF BY NOW
OVER-FAMILIAR *NOIR*
TERRITORY.

But critical sticks and stones were of no consequence to their target, who was going his own, increasingly independent, way, resisting an invitation from playwright Tennessee Williams and director Elia Kazan to play Stanley Kowalski in *A Streetcar Named Desire* on stage. Had he accepted, his decision might well have changed the course of two careers, his own and that of Marlon Brando.

With Burt's status and financial prospects growing steadily, he and Harold Hecht decided to take the plunge and realize their dream of going into production for themselves. They formed Hecht-Norma Productions (the 'Norma' so named for Burt's wife). It was a ground-breaking decision, the first major actor-producer set-up since the famous founding of United Artists by Pickford, Fairbanks, Chaplin and D.W. Griffith in 1919, since when only James Cagney had taken a step in that direction. Now, in time, others, notably Kirk Douglas, would follow suit, thus contributing to the eventual demise of the studio system.

Lancaster went into the production business with the clearly stated objective of making quality pictures. 'We were trying to develop a continuing company, and we were not primarily concerned with making money; our reason was the need for independence. I felt that Hollywood couldn't go on doing a lot of what was pure pap, as well as a lot of good films that were purely entertaining. People had to be given some of the realities of life... films in their own way are history-making. Like all good art, they illuminate something... This doesn't mean that all films should be very serious things. There's a great deal of room for the pleasant fun film...'

Fine words (albeit with several escape clauses) and sincerely meant, and over the next few years Hecht-Lancaster would honour the philosophy with an eclectic mixture of 'fun' films and more serious, even literary, material. Their first venture, however, was certainly a retrograde step, both in terms of their objectives and in relation to Burt's growing image problem as a *film noir* actor.

Made with borrowed money, *Kiss the Blood Off My Hands* offered a lurid, attention-grabbing title and exceptionally good fake London

settings. For the rest, it was the 'pure pap' that Lancaster was so eager to banish, and which saw him as yet another ambiguous not-so-tough tough guy. He played a war-scarred Canadian marine, an ex-POW, with a dangerously explosive temper, who kills a man in a London pub fight and goes on the run. He finds refuge with a nurse (a frightfully refined, oddly cast Joan Fontaine), but they fall into the clutches of a thuggish blackmailer, played by that fine purveyor of the rough-edged sinister, Robert Newton, who, in the context of the ludicrous screenplay and Norman Foster's pedestrian direction, tipped over into near-caricature.

Released by Universal, the film failed to generate much excitement or hoped-for profit, and was not an auspicious launch for Hecht-Norma. It did, however, bring its founders face to face with the realities of production problems. Fontaine turned out to be newly pregnant, and subsequently needed almost a fortnight off to nurse a bad cold; rarely for Los Angeles, rain at the wrong times played havoc with exterior shooting and Newton, an insecure man with a drinking problem, was upset by the constant changes in schedule.

For Burt it was now back to the business of being a jobbing actor, a not unpleasing prospect since the job in question was the last of the three under his agreement with Mark Hellinger. The film, *Criss Cross*, was yet another *noir*, with Robert Siodmak again engaged to direct, but the project suffered a terrible blow with the sudden death of the forty-four-year-old Hellinger. This left the artistic control in the hands of Universal, who ordered rewrites that resulted in what Burt described as a 'rehashed chow of a script'. Siodmak and Lancaster, obliged to go ahead, did so with reluctance and as best they could, but, despite the eloquently moody camerawork of Franz Planer, one of the finest lighting cameramen in the business, *Criss Cross* was no more than another formula *noir* (though surprisingly highly regarded by aficionados). Burt played yet another victim of a duplicitous woman (Yvonne de Carlo) and a ruthless criminal (Dan Duryea). For the eagle-eyed, there's a blink-and-you'll-miss-it appearance by the young Tony Curtis, dancing in a club with De Carlo — the humble debut of a future star who would later share honours with Lancaster.

In the absence of Bosley Crowther from the *New York Times*, critic Thomas Pryor wrote, 'It should not be surprising that his [Lancaster's] performance is competent, for he has been working at the same type of

ANOTHER ILL-FATED *NOIR* VICTIM FOR BURT IN *CRISS CROSS*, WITH YVONNE DE CARLO AS THE LADY IN THE CASE. THE FILM REUNITED THE STAR WITH ROBERT SIODMAK, BUT IN LESS HAPPY CIRCUMSTANCES THAN THOSE OF *THE KILLERS*.

Burt decided to take a break from the rigours of filming and experience life as an acrobat on the road once more.

role for some time.' More point-edly, the *Herald Tribune* noted that 'Lancaster is almost forced into a nearby parody of his previous dumb brute portrayals.' Clearly, something would have to be done to correct this growing impression.

Meanwhile Burt's friend and former partner Nick Cravat was in Los Angeles acting as his private fitness trainer and regularly working out with him on the horizontal bars. In November 1948, Burt decided to take a break from the rigours of filming and experience life as an acrobat on the road once more. He and Nick revived their act for a fortnight, touring with the Cole Brothers circus, but this time they travelled by specially fitted-out luxury train, and were paid $10,000 per week.

Then it was back to Hal Wallis and another macho role in *Rope of Sand*. In an unsubtle bid to recapture the heady success of *Casablanca*, the producer rounded up Paul Henreid, Claude Rains and Peter Lorre, while, as the lady in the case, French actress Corinne Calvet made a somewhat uncomfortable American debut.

BURT AND NICK CRAVAT RETURNED TO THE BIG TOP AT THE COLE BROTHERS CIRCUS IN LATE 1948. THIS TIME IT WAS FOR FUN.

At least this was a departure from *noir*, an improbable pot-boiler about diamond mining, set in Hollywood's rather fanciful idea of South Africa. The plot had Burt as a big-game hunter, heroically outwitting a smoothly scheming Rains and a chillingly sadistic Henreid in a complicated hunt for hidden gems. It was more 'pure pap', an adult-flavoured version of a Saturday serial action adventure but, seen today, hilariously entertaining.

THE TOUGH ADVENTURER
OF *ROPE OF SAND* PLANS
HIS REVENGE AGAINST THE
VILLAINS. LANCASTER
WITH PETER LORRE.

Rope of Sand was released in August 1949, a month after the birth of Burt and Norma's second child, Susan Elizabeth, and, as biographer Robert Windeler expresses it, was 'the last occasion on which Burt Lancaster did an acting job simply because Hal Wallis said he should'.

A new decade was on the horizon and, with it, a new phase in the career of Lancaster, who, despite a generally mediocre filmography, had achieved the status of a megastar.

Flying high

CHAPTER THREE

Nineteen-fifty was a key year for Burt Lancaster. After the release of *Kiss the Blood Off My Hands*, Thomas M. Pryor wrote a piece in the *New York Times* suggesting that 'The process of humanizing Burt Lancaster is not going to be easy... to develop fully as an actor and to come over to the right side of society he will have to make a break someday, for there are only so many variations on the theme of being misunderstood, and Mr Lancaster has just about exhausted them.'

With nine films (excluding a brief sketch in Paramount's *Variety Girl*) behind him, Burt had proved himself eminently bankable, but he knew that he must throw off the dead-end shackles of type-casting if he were to achieve the degree of critical and commercial success he so passionately desired.

The original segment of the Wallis contract had run its course in 1949, but, disagreements and differences of approach between star and director notwithstanding, it seemed in both their best interests to renew. This time, however, the terms were more favourable to Lancaster, allowing him a larger measure of freedom to work elsewhere.

Hecht-Norma had not attempted another production since *Kiss the Blood Off My Hands*. The time was now clearly ripe to start living up to their aspirations, and they were given the wherewithal to do so when Hecht negotiated a deal with Warner Bros., whereby the studio agreed to back Hecht-Norma as producers in exchange for a commitment from Lancaster to appear, as actor only, in one Warner Bros. production for each Hecht-Norma production. It was a singular and fruitful contract.

> '**There are only so many variations on the theme of being misunderstood, and Mr Lancaster has just about exhausted them.**'

DARDO, A SMILING HERO IN THE FAIRBANKS-FLYNN TRADITION. *THE FLAME AND THE ARROW*, HECHT-NORMA'S SECOND PRODUCTION, WAS HUGELY SUCCESSFUL.

DARDO DEFENDS HIMSELF
AGAINST THE VILLAIN'S
SWORD.

It was at Warners that Errol Flynn had popularly and profitably resuscitated the swashbuckling adventure in the Fairbanks tradition with *Captain Blood* (1935), *The Adventures of Robin Hood* (1938) and *The Sea Hawk* (1940). By 1950 Flynn was more or less washed up and there was a gap for this particular brand of action hero just waiting to be filled. It was well known that Lancaster's previous profession had been that of circus acrobat – a useful provenance for the publicity departments, but Hollywood producers had thus far signally failed to capitalize on his athletic skills. Now, at thirty-seven, he was given his opportunity, and took it with breathtaking zest and vigour.

Hecht and Lancaster had acquired Waldo Salt's screenplay *The Flame and the Arrow*, and taken it to Columbia, who wanted the star to make a picture for them. It turned out that they were after another characteristic Lancaster crime movie, so Hecht sent the property to Jack Warner, whose immediate enthusiasm was fuelled by the fact that the studio still had the sets from *The Adventures of Robin Hood*. Harold and Burt were quick to see the economic advantages in this.

The Flame and the Arrow was genre hokum, set in a typically Hollywoodian no-man's land that, on this occasion, masqueraded as eleventh-century Lombardy. The film concerned the conflict between the evil Ulrich of Hesse and the Italian peasants he tyrannically rules on behalf of Frederick Barbarossa. At the centre of events is the outlaw Dardo (Lancaster), famed for his marksmanship with a bow and arrow and much loved by the local populace. Deserted by his wife in favour of the rich and powerful Ulrich, Dardo lives in a mountain hide-out with his adored small son and his faithful sidekick Piccolo, an extraordinary mute, played by Nick Cravat, making his film debut.

Open rebellion breaks out when Ulrich forcibly removes Dardo's son to live at court with his mother. How Dardo outwits and disposes of Ulrich, gets his son back, and finds love with the Princess of Hesse (Virginia Mayo), whom he has taken hostage, is the stuff of which this *Boy's Own Paper* derring-do, with resonances of *Robin Hood*, is made.

The film is a delight, with Salt's classy retread of formula territory tightly constructed and laced with well-judged tongue-in-cheek humour. ('I always said we should have been acrobats,' murmurs a grinning Burt to Cravat after a marvellous action set-piece.) Since the film's

DARDO PREPARES
TO CATCH HIS LOYAL
SIDEKICK, PICCOLO
(NICK CRAVAT), DURING
THE MOVIE'S CLIMACTIC
ACTION SEQUENCE.
BURT AND NICK
PERFORMED THEIR OWN
STUNTS.

sole intention is to entertain, it requires no more suspension of disbelief than any good fairy tale and has held up well.

Directed with brio by Jacques Tourneur, a versatile craftsman of a high order, the film was a big-earning success that unleashed a new Burt Lancaster. The excellent colour quality brought the blue eyes, blond hair and famous flashing smile into full and beguiling focus, while his magnificent physique was given its full due. Most impressively, Burt scaled mountain slopes and castle walls, leapt from turrets, swung from chandeliers, indulged in swordplay, and put on a balancing act with Cravat. And it *was* Burt. Where most men would defer to the approach of middle age, he eschewed the use of stunt men and proved his athletic credentials.

Despite Lancaster's resistance to publicity campaigning, he and Cravat promoted the film by touring their act. Warners, in a fit of promotional zeal, offered $1 million to anyone who could prove that the actor had not performed his acrobat's feats himself. Inevitably, a stunt double came forward to claim the prize, but lost his case when it was proved that he had done no more than stand in for a couple of long shots.

With *The Flame and the Arrow*, Burt had not only realized his boyhood dream of emulating his hero, Douglas Fairbanks, but found what had, despite his box-office appeal, thus far eluded him: universal affection. And in purely practical terms, the film's enormous success with critics (even Bosley Crowther enthused) and public alike put his production company on the map, paving the way for more ambitious projects.

Aside from the exhilarating physicality of Burt's Dardo, he displayed a lighter touch than hitherto — affectionate, hail-fellow-well-met and mildly joky, preceding another change of mood with his next film, this time as actor only, on loan to Twentieth Century-Fox. Robert Riskin scripted *Mister 880*, a good-hearted piece of sentimental whimsy in which Burt found himself on the right side of the law as a US Treasury investigator, or T-Man, specializing in nailing counterfeit-

There are forced moments as he struggles for the smoothness that came so naturally to actors like James Stewart.

ers. Called in to a curious case that has been baffling the New York authorities for a decade — the sporadic passing of modest sums in fake one-dollar bills — he traces the source of one transaction to a pretty United Nations interpreter (Dorothy McGuire), falls for her, and finally discovers what the audience has guessed from the outset: the culprit is a poor, kind-hearted, and very elderly junk dealer (Edmund Gwenn), who lives with his lovable dog in the same apartment block as Miss McGuire.

With direction by Edmund Goulding, the cultivated veteran of many a classic, and a rave from *Variety*, who predicted that it couldn't miss at the box office, the movie still sank virtually without trace. The era of charming sentimentality had faded, and audiences clearly preferred Burt as action man. None the less, for Burt-watchers, it is interesting to see his efforts to broaden his range. There are forced moments as he struggles for the smoothness that came so naturally to actors like James Stewart (who would have been perfect casting), but his hard work achieved a convincing and likeable 'establishment' image.

Hal Wallis was now approached for Burt's services by MGM, the only major studio for whom the actor had not yet worked. Wallis had planned to cast him in *Dark City*, but the MGM offer was too good to turn down, and it was thus that Charlton Heston, a new Wallis contract

LEFT: LANCASTER IN THE
WIDE OPEN SPACES OF HIS
FIRST WESTERN,
VENGEANCE VALLEY,
MADE ON LOAN-OUT TO
MGM.

player, came to his first major role, while Burt was initiated into a genre obviously suited to his personality and physique, the Western.

Directed by Richard Thorpe, *Vengeance Valley* dealt in family drama rather than saloon shoot-outs or Indian wars. Burt played a cattle-ranch foreman, the loyal, hardworking foster son of Ray Collins, who protects Collins' no-good real son (Robert Walker) from the consequences of his sins, which include getting a decent girl pregnant and allowing the vengeful suspicion of her brothers to fall on Burt. There is an eventual showdown and justice is done, *en route* to which the film offers a spectacular cattle round-up by way of a set-piece against which the climactic drama unfolds. Though the movie is tautly scripted and well acted, the direction is run of the mill, and an air of predictability hovering over the film robs it of tension. As one commentator put it, more soap opera than horse opera.

A better opportunity came to Burt with his next film, back at Warner Bros., who had for some time held the rights to the autobiography of the great athlete Jim Thorpe. The naturally fleet-footed Thorpe grew up on an Indian reservation in Oklahoma and discovered his sportsman's

RIGHT: EXPRESSING A
FORCEFUL OPINION ON THE
SET OF *JIM THORPE –
ALL-AMERICAN.*
CO-STAR PHYLLIS
THAXTER IS SEATED ON
THE RIGHT.

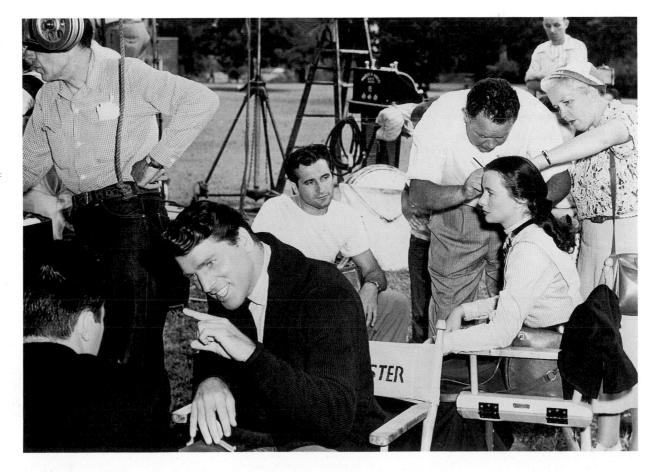

THE MULTI-TALENTED
OLYMPIC ATHLETICS CHAM-
PION JIM THORPE FOUND
A SECOND STRING TO HIS
BOW AS A SPECTACULAR
FOOTBALL PLAYER, BUT HIS
CAREER AND HIS LIFE
ENDED IN RUINS.

gifts while studying at Carlile Indian College. He proved as talented at football and baseball as he was at track and field sports, but it was in the latter that he represented his country at the 1912 Olympics in Stockholm, where, extraordinarily, he won both the Pentathlon and Decathlon, setting new records in each. A national hero, he was subsequently stripped of his medals and struck from the record books when it was learned that he had played baseball for money a couple of years earlier. He turned professional ball-player but, frustrated in his ambitions and embittered by the circumstances of his life, which included the death of a much-loved small son, he sank into personal decline, drinking and drifting, and found work as a Hollywood extra during the forties, generally as a stock Indian.

The script that was fashioned from Thorpe's life story offered a sentimentalized account of the events, reducing the athlete's three wives and six children to one wife and one child (the son who died) and kept Thorpe off the skids for most of the film, treating him for the most part as sympathetic hero-figure and victim of circumstance. The aspects of racial prejudice in the Indian's life were a factor in attracting Lancaster to the project. They were only marginally touched on in the finished product, but the implications were none the less clear. For all that it is sanitized, the film is affecting and, as directed with high competence by Michael Curtiz, and in its handling of athletics and football, remains rightly

Lancaster was alternating work with little motive other than financial gain, with films of higher aspiration.

acknowledged as one of Hollywood's best-ever sports movies.

Thorpe himself was brought in as adviser. Burt recalled that 'My only personal contact with him during the filming was when he did drop-kicking. He came out of the stands and tried to teach me. It was sort of touching. His life had gone to pot.'

But with *Jim Thorpe — All-American* (released in the UK as *Man of Bronze*) Thorpe's tragedy became Lancaster's triumph. Although by no means looking like 'a man of bronze' — only the blond locks were darkened in the interests of authenticity — Lancaster gave an impressive performance, restrained and sensitive in the early stages, capturing the young Thorpe's innocence at being thrown, reluctantly, into an academic and sporting world of which he had neither knowledge nor understanding. Thorpe's gradual disintegration (and fictitious redemption) was well paced and convincing, with the actor revealing the interior man, and at no time trying to compensate for his lack of resemblance to

the real Thorpe by artificial tricks or make-up. Echoing a complimentary response from *Variety*, A.H. Weiler in the *New York Times* considered that 'The Warner Bros. could not have assigned a better man to the title role than Burt Lancaster. He is equipped physically and, what is more important, professionally, for the job...'

For their next picture, Hecht-Norma finally reached agreement at Columbia. *Ten Tall Men* was a Foreign Legion actioner with Burt in charge of a band of men who must defend their headquarters from Arab attack. In effect a swashbuckler in the sand, the film acted as an inconsequential bridge between *The Flame and the Arrow* and the producers' next, *The Crimson Pirate*, employing salient plot elements common to both: an adversary within (Burt's less than sympathetic commanding officer), an enemy without (the Arab chieftain, played by Gilbert Roland with hammy suavity) and the kidnapping of the chief's daughter (Jody Lawrence) by Burt's men, leading, predictably, to romance. The movie is a vigorous near-parody of the genres from which it draws, raising laughs while supplying heroics – an old-fashioned yarn, custom-built for Lancaster and made with both eyes firmly on the cash register. It opened in October 1951 and, as hoped, proved extremely profitable.

Money was now an important factor for Lancaster. With a steadily expanding family to support – his second daughter, Joanna, had been born in July – and the substantial overheads of Hecht-Norma Productions to consider, a pattern was emerging wherein he was alternating work with little motive other than financial gain with films of higher aspiration. He himself once remarked, 'It happens to everybody at some time or another – even me – you need money.'

The same year, Harold and Burt made their next film for Warner Bros. Taking their cue from the popularity of *The Flame and the Arrow* and *Ten Tall Men*, they chose another swashbuckler, this time an overt homage to Fairbanks and Flynn, even down to slashing the mast as Doug had famously done in *The Black Pirate* (1920) and Errol had attempted to repeat in *Against All Flags* (1952). From an original screenplay by Roland Kibbee (who co-scripted *Ten Tall Men*), *The Crimson Pirate* was an action-packed and inventive spoof, supplying some genuinely exciting sequences, such as a hazardous chase sequence at sea.

The movie's opening sets the tone as pirate captain Vallo (Lancaster),

ABOVE: THE SMILING FACE OF THE FOREIGN LEGION-NAIRE IN *TEN TALL MEN*. HECHT AND LANCASTER SMILED ALL THE WAY TO THE BANK.

LEFT: THE TEDIUM OF WAITING AROUND ON LOCATION.

aloft the rigging of his ship, addresses the audience directly: '…You've been shanghaied aboard for the last cruise of the *Crimson Pirate*. A long, long time ago in the far, far Caribbean. Remember, in a pirate ship in pirate waters, in a pirate world. Ask no questions, believe only what you see. No! Believe only half of what you see.'

The complicated story that follows the buccaneer's exhortation essentially concerns Vallo's exploits when, for a sum of gold, he agrees to take leave of absence from his piracy to quell a revolt against the Spanish overlords of a small Caribbean island. Once there, he falls for the daughter (Eva Bartok) of the people's leader, and switches allegiance, thereby causing a near-mutiny in his own ranks. The deliciously tongue-in-cheek antics of Vallo, his sidekicks James Hayter and Nick Cravat (mute again and marvellous) and the island's resident inventor, who creates a primitive submarine for their escape, are ingenious and funny. (Highlights include Lancaster and his cronies in unselfconscious and hilariously ridiculous drag as island maidens.)

The film opened to critical approval in August 1952. A.H. Weiler in the *New York Times* not only appreciated the humour and the acrobatics of Nick Cravat, but found Lancaster 'truly a picture pirate. A blond, smiling, muscular and agile athlete…' The film was a massive hit. Good humour was a major key to its success but, ironically, it had been filmed in an atmosphere of tension and acrimony.

The Crimson Pirate marked Burt's first assignment to be shot outside the United States. A combination of lower production costs and frozen assets made Europe an attractive proposition for Warner Bros., who chose the Bay of Naples and the magical little island of Ischia as outdoor locations, while interiors were filmed at Teddington Studios just outside London. (It was during this time that Burt consolidated an enduring passion for Italy.) Lancaster was reunited with Robert Siodmak, but the star showed none of his earlier respect for the experienced filmmaker. He claimed to have invested five years of effort into realizing the project

and was determined to have his own way in the making of it. His reputation for giving orders to his fellow actors and attempting to dictate to directors was now an established fact of his professional conduct and, although it was motivated as much by passionate commitment as by a large ego, caused friction.

On this occasion tension ran high as Lancaster openly queried or overruled Siodmak's decisions, even, on one much-reported occasion, calling the director a 'silly old has-been' in full hearing of cast and crew. Burt's explosive temper was periodically vented on the other actors, even his friend Nick Cravat, with whom he managed to fight. In his defence, it is clear that his all-consuming involvement in the film and his determination to ensure a successful production sparked off his outbursts. He later said of the film's making, 'I designed all the action sequences... all the comedy stuff. I worked with a comedy writer [Roland Kibbee] as well as with Siodmak himself. And, as a matter of fact, the whole last part of the film, the fight on the ship which runs eighteen minutes of screen time, with all the gags and jokes, was shot by a writer and myself while Siodmak was in London shooting interiors...'

Norma and Burt stayed together beyond the natural term of their affection only for the sake of their children.

He was also quoted as saying, in what amounted to a rare hint of apology, 'I like to find out how the camera works, then I can try for the best effect in what I'm doing. I want to know the director's angle on things as well. I know it's difficult. But I'm like that, restless and strung up inside when I'm working. I am searching for something and I haven't found it yet.'

Off-screen, too, he was capable of unpleasant behaviour, often causing embarrassment to others while seemingly able to forget the incident moments later. Writer Sheilah Graham, an admirer of the actor but not, once she had been on the receiving end of his tongue, of the man, recorded in her book *Scratch an Actor: Confessions of a Hollywood Columnist*, 'Lancaster's terrible temper is well known in Hollywood. He can restrain himself for the screen, and this held-back anger is very effective in his films. But in real life when he is annoyed, his eruptions are alarming.'

The Lancaster family image at the time was a happy one — it only emerged years later that his marriage was under severe strain from quite early on and that Norma and Burt stayed together beyond the natural term of their affection only for the sake of their children. And indeed

HILARITY AMIDST THE SWASH AND BUCKLE: VALLO (BURT, SEATED CENTRE) AND CRONIES (CRAVAT SEATED RIGHT) PASS THEMSELVES OFF AS ISLAND MAIDENS.

ABOVE: THE LANCASTER
FAMILY IN 1954. FROM
LEFT TO RIGHT, JOANNA,
BURT, SUSAN, NORMA,
JAMES AND BILLY.
RIGHT: INTRODUCING
DAUGHTER JOANNA TO
THE CAMERAS.

Lancaster was a loving and concerned father who would have the kids visit on the set but, to the chagrin of the publicists, refused to put on any kind of a show with them for the press. His extramarital affairs were conducted with discretion and escaped the prying eyes of the tabloid journalists, and he lived a quiet life, eschewing large social gatherings (he behaved extremely badly at a party given by Harold Hecht which he had been reluctant to attend) in favour of home life, golf and bridge.

With *The Crimson Pirate* safely out of the way, there were commitments to fulfil for Hal Wallis, and he agreed to appear in a sketch on NBC-TV's *Colgate Comedy Hour* with Wallis 'properties' Dean Martin and Jerry Lewis. This was his debut in the medium from whose drama writers he would draw producer's inspiration, but in which he would not work until his twilight years. Meanwhile, having voluntarily played second fiddle to Barbara Stanwyck five years earlier in *Sorry, Wrong Number*, he was far more interested in persuading the producer, whose judgement he had so delighted in maligning, to allow him to do so again, this time to Broadway actress Shirley Booth, recreating her award-winning performance in *Come Back, Little Sheba*.

Lancaster, still outstandingly fit at nearly forty, and as handsome as

ever, was hardly ideal casting for the part of Doc Delaney, a burnt-out, disillusioned alcoholic trapped in a compromise marriage to the once-pretty Lola, whose own disillusionment and frustration have reduced her to a slatternly chatterbox, taking refuge in radio soap operas, unable to come to terms with her guilt at having lost the baby that forced Doc to marry her, and mourning the disappearance of her great love, her little dog Sheba.

Determined to retain Miss Booth, a newcomer to film, Wallis needed the ballast of a box-office name for Doc (Sidney Blackmer had created the role), and Lancaster, recognizing the kind of serious challenge he was burning to meet, determined that the part should be his, despite the misgivings in which he shared.

AN ANXIOUS LOLA DELANEY (SHIRLEY BOOTH) TRIES TO COMMUNICATE WITH HER TROUBLED HUSBAND DOC (LANCASTER) IN *COME BACK, LITTLE SHEBA.*

Later he gave two conflicting accounts of his discussions with the producer. In January 1953, weeks after the film's release, he told the *New York Times* that 'My role as Doc gives me the best opportunity to act I've ever had. But, you know, I didn't even want to look at the script when Mr Wallis asked me to read it. I had been playing rough-and-tumble action roles for so long that I couldn't imagine myself as a disillusioned ex-alcoholic married to a pitiful frump...'

His other recollection would seem to be more accurate. Wallis told Burt he was too young for the part. 'I had to agree with Wallis really, because the man in *Come Back, Little Sheba* should have been about sixty. But it was a part I wanted to play more than any other I ever got close to. Doc Delaney is the most human, if imperfect, kind of guy ever written into a play or script. I prevailed on Wallis, I said, "I understand this character. I'd like to play it. Now, we both know that it's Shirley's film, she's got the lead. But if I can do a respectable job in it, I will lend some weight to the box office for you." '

Like all Lancaster's best work, *Come Back, Little Sheba* is an interior performance, controlled and subtle.

It was an almost exact rerun of the *Sorry, Wrong Number* discussion. His arguments are amply demonstrative of his high ambition, combined with arrogance but accompanied by a realistic appraisal of the situation – and, on the plus side, his ability to detect quality in a script, admire another artist and defer gracefully when necessary. ('Shirley,' he remarked, 'is an inspiration.')

In his autobiography Wallis writes, 'It was difficult for this huge, virile man to look like a weakling. We dressed Burt in a sloppy, shapeless button-up sweater, padded his figure to flab out his trim waistline...' They also greyed his hair, gave him pale, ageing make-up and encouraged the hollow-chested stoop he adopted for the role. Interestingly, Wallis continues, 'Burt went along with everything. Many male stars would have resisted, fearing that so unattractive an appearance might damage them in the eyes of their fans. But the good side of his cool confidence made any such loss of popularity unthinkable.'

The central focus of William Inge's play and, to only slightly less an extent, Ketti Frings' screen adaptation, is firmly on the well-meaning, irritating Lola Delaney, but the role of Doc, whose suppressed emotions are unleashed to violent crisis point by the arrival of a pretty college girl to lodge in his home, and the presence of her sexually predatory and conceited boyfriend, is substantial. The film version of this bleak,

powerful and poignant drama (well directed by Daniel Mann, who had staged it on Broadway) leaves the Delaneys — and the audience — on a note of hope, but insufficient to give it wide box-office appeal.

For Burt Lancaster, however, it was a milestone. He worked extremely hard to bring credibility to his performance, so much so that he almost overcame his obvious physical miscasting and his own technical limitations as an actor. Like all his best work, it is an interior performance, controlled and subtle, with his natural bullishness only breaking out in the scenes of drunken violence, where they are not inappropriate. Most noticeably, there is a painful, touching sweetness in those moments where he attempts to be kind to Lola.

Variety expressed unreserved enthusiasm for the film and noted that Lancaster brought 'an unsuspected talent to his role'. The actor's traditionally critical adversary, Bosley Crowther of the *New York Times*, conceded that 'the excellence of Mr Lancaster as the frustrated, inarticulate spouse, weak-willed and sweetly passive, should not be overlooked'. The *New Yorker* and the London *Sunday Times* (Dilys Powell) joined in the accolades, but *Time* magazine felt that Burt's performance 'frequently makes the character seem wooden rather than frustrated'; and in Britain Lindsay Anderson, writing for *Sight and Sound*, considered that 'Lancaster is an actor of instinctive sensitivity, whose playing has always had a certain gentleness and sensibility. But his range is limited, and this difficult part goes beyond it.'

HAVING BROKEN HIS
ABSTINENCE AND GONE ON
A DRUNKEN BINGE, THE
CRAZED DOC TRIES TO
ATTACK LOLA.
THE FILM REPRESENTED
LANCASTER'S BIGGEST
CHALLENGE TO THAT DATE.

To Lancaster himself, however, the achievement of playing a shambling wreck counted as something of a triumph. And he could share in the reflected glory of the unforgettable Shirley Booth, who won best actress at Cannes and the top Oscar to add to her Broadway Tony award.

From the challenging heights of *Come Back, Little Sheba*, Burt tumbled to the forgettable lows of two appearances for Warner Bros. *South Sea Woman*, released in June 1953, followed the antic adventures of two marines (Lancaster and Chuck Connors) in the Pacific, both caught up with an island-hopping glamour gal (Virginia Mayo). It was played for laughs that audiences clearly didn't share, and though Burt seemed to enjoy himself on screen as he tore bar-rooms apart and took on the Japanese fleet single-handed, it added nothing to his prestige. Without, as legend has it, even having to change out of his sailor suit from that film, he crossed to a neighbouring studio to make an uncredited, one-line guest appearance in *Three Sailors and a Girl*, a feeble musical released

WAITING AMIDST A
JUNGLE OF CAMERAS FOR
THE BEACH SCENES TO
COMMENCE IN
FROM HERE TO ETERNITY.

in November. Both appearances discharged contractual obligations to Warners, leaving one more production to be delivered by Hecht-Norma. But first, Lancaster left for Schofield army barracks in Hawaii, and by far the most prestigious film and role of his career to that date.

In 1953, during the typically sweltering New York summer, *From Here to Eternity* opened at the Capitol Theater on Broadway, with neither publicity nor a première. But the jungle drum was beating. By midnight the queues were still around the block, and an extra performance was laid on at one in the morning. One of the major films of the 1950s, it brought a shower of critical praise and excited universal audience enthusiasm.

James Jones' best-selling 860-page novel had caused something of a sensation with its uncompromising portrayal of army life in Hawaii prior to, but culminating in, the bombing of Pearl Harbor. Generously laced with sex, brutality and foul language, the story takes a hard and truthful look at the lives and temperaments of career officers and enlisted men, sparing no detail of the cruelty practised by some under the sometimes acquiescent, sometimes unseeing eyes of others. Jones also pays tribute to the brotherhood of decent men, and treats his female characters with sympathy and understanding. It is a monumental novel which required a skilful screenplay and the highest quality of director, cast and crew to save it from becoming just another army pot-boiler.

The film rights had been bought by the most independent and ruthless of Hollywood's moguls, Columbia's Harry Cohn, for the then high price of $82,000. Daniel Taradash came up with a suitably impressive screenplay and Fred Zinnemann was hired to direct. The Viennese-born Zinnemann at that stage had won Academy Award nominations for *The*

Search (1948), Montgomery Clift's debut feature, and for *High Noon* (1952), and had made Marlon Brando's first film, *The Men* (1950). A man of fine taste and judgement with an expert eye for casting, Zinnemann was exactly the right choice to do justice to the material.

The main plot of *From Here to Eternity* concerns the sensitive Private Prewitt (Montgomery Clift), an inspirational bugler and a brilliant boxer who refuses to fight since the death of a buddy in the ring. He is systematically victimized by the brass, who try to force him to box for the unit, and forbid him the bugler's position because he won't give in. Prewitt's best friend, Maggio (Frank Sinatra), an irrepressible rebel, falls foul of the sadistic sergeant (Ernest Borgnine) in command of the stockade. He, too, is victimized, provoked until he ends up in the man's charge, and is brutalized to the point of death.

THE FIRST CHARGED MEETING BETWEEN SERGEANT WARDEN AND THE CAPTAIN'S BEAUTIFUL WIFE, KAREN HOLMES (DEBORAH KERR).

The men's superior officer, the master sergeant answerable in turn to a weak and corrupt captain, is Sergeant Milt Warden (Lancaster), well described by Mel Schuster as a man 'who runs the company, whose *home* is the army; who *seems* to confront all problems *physically*, but who stands by his convictions even when it hurts, and who is sensitive enough to find love in a situation he had gotten into merely for casual sex.'

The love affair is, of course, the now legendary one with Deborah Kerr, whose climax among the waves on a Honolulu beach sent shock waves through critics and audiences throughout the world, so daring did it seem in its time. In Zinnemann's view, 'Burt Lancaster seemed to be the best choice for the part of the master sergeant. This was type-casting. Not only did he have the right authority and weight, but more importantly there was a chemistry between him and Deborah, and the combination worked out well, especially in the beach scene...' (That 'chemistry', over the years, gave rise to persistent but unsubstantiated rumours that Kerr and Lancaster had an off-screen involvement — one of several such bits of gossip, sometimes true, that surrounded the actor.)

As Sergeant Warden in *From Here to Eternity*, he sat in the skin of the role, carrying himself like a career soldier.

Lancaster more than justified Zinnemann's faith. For the first, but very far from the last, time in his career, his own military training came into its own. He sat in the skin of the role, carrying himself like a career soldier, and, under the director's careful and co-operative guidance, modulated and shaded his performance to perfection. The authority and weight which Fred Zinnemann detected had not previously been exploited, but would now become a striking feature of Lancaster's best films and performances.

Burt kept his argumentative on-set shenanigans to an acceptable minimum, perhaps because, as he said, 'Many directors, when questioned by an actor, feel they're losing control. Zinnemann encourages it.'

The actor held his own in a collection of absolutely outstanding performances, not least that of Montgomery Clift, whom he later called 'the hardest-working actor I've ever known', although there was little love lost between them. Clift received $150,000 for his work, Lancaster $120,000 and Frank Sinatra $8,000. Practically on the skids when the film was announced, Sinatra had begged for the role of Maggio, offering to do it for nothing, and got it when Eli Wallach, already cast, pulled out. He gave an unforgettable performance and was rewarded with the

THE CLIMACTIC LOVE
SCENES ON A HAWAIIAN
BEACH IN *FROM HERE TO
ETERNITY* CAUSED A
FURORE WHEN THE FILM
WAS RELEASED.

Best Supporting Actor Oscar and a new lease of professional life. Donna Reed, as Clift's nightclub hostess girlfriend, was voted Best Supporting Actress, but Miss Kerr, for whom the film broke new ground, lost out to Audrey Hepburn, making her debut in *Roman Holiday*. As well as grossing $18 million worldwide at the box office, *From Here to Eternity* garnered rave reviews and thirteen Oscar nominations, winning eight of them, including Best Picture.

A haunting, hard-hitting drama, it remains as compellingly watchable, engrossing and disturbing today as it was then. For Lancaster, it signified an entry into a higher echelon of screen acting, and brought him his first Academy Award nomination. (He lost to William Holden in *Stalag 17*.)

Though probably in a position to do almost anything he wished after this success, Burt moved straight into making the third film owed to Hecht-Norma under their Warner Bros. deal. *His Majesty O'Keefe*, directed by Byron Haskin from an original screenplay by Borden Chase and James Hill, proved rather a curious film. Burt starred as a sea captain who, after a mutiny, is washed ashore on an island presided over by an agent (André Morell) for a German company that buys the local copra. His opportunistic instincts lead him to try to take over the enterprise, which means wooing the natives and outwitting the Germans, involving him in seafaring adventures, various kinds of mutiny and marriage to a youthful South Seas beauty (Joan Rice).

The film is curious in that, by the end, O'Keefe has won over the natives and been made into their saviour and king, but there is a definite implication that his strength, power and ego will see him drift into megalomania rather than the enlightened humanitarianism the audience has been expecting.

En route to its ending, it gave its star plenty of opportunity to demonstrate his strength and agility. Photographed by Otto Heller in glorious colour, the lush location (Viti Levu, the largest of the Fiji islands) adds atmosphere to what is an unimportant, strictly commercial movie. Conditions, apparently, were not easy, mainly owing to the intense heat and humidity. In an interview, Lancaster remarked that 'it was so tough working in the humidity that one day I actually watched fungus grow on my clothes'. He had, however, taken Norma and the children with him, making a family holiday out of the experience.

Released in early 1954, *His Majesty O'Keefe* proved moderately successful. It was also the last production from Hecht-Norma, heralding the beginning of a unique deal with United Artists and a consistently ambitious phase in Burt Lancaster's career.

TAKING THE SUN DURING THE FILMING OF *HIS MAJESTY O'KEEFE* WITH BILLY, SUSAN AND, ON ACTOR CHARLES HORVATH'S LAP, JIMMY.

The power game

By 1950, United Artists, originally founded as the stars' own studio to launch productions free of control by the moguls, had undergone a series of financial and management convulsions and was on the verge of bankruptcy. In 1951 UA was taken over by Arthur Krim and Robert Benjamin, who revitalized the studio by means of production deals with independent producers, somewhat in the company's founding spirit.

In the early years of the decade Burt Lancaster was one of the few newer male stars in a commanding position, while MCA, under the presidency of Lew Wasserman, had become the most powerful talent agency in America. And it was to Lancaster, represented by Wasserman, that Krim and Benjamin turned in search of a star to spearhead their new push for commercial and artistic success. A deal, to take effect after the completion of Hecht-Norma's Warner Bros. commit-

Twenty years later Burt said of *Apache*:

'As I have done many times in my life,

I sold my soul to the Devil.'

ments, had been brokered in June 1953. A multiple-picture contract, it gave Burt and Harold Hecht not only full finance for five productions, but seventy-five per cent of the profits and an overhead allowance to pay for the development of scripts. In addition, Krim was levered into certain concessions on distribution fees — concessions so exceptional that they had to be kept confidential and were referred to within UA as the 'Lancaster terms'.

The 'Norma' was dropped from Harold and Burt's company name and it was as Hecht-Lancaster that they embarked on the first phase of their new deal. They began with *Apache*, the second of Burt's thirteen Westerns, and the first of four pictures he would make with director Robert Aldrich, then a comparative newcomer to feature-film directing,

LONE DEFENDER OF HIS LAND: THE PROUD WARRIOR MASSAI IN ROBERT ALDRICH'S *APACHE*, THE FIRST FILM UNDER THE HECHT-LANCASTER BANNER.

THE CAPTIVE MASSAI
STEALTHILY MAKING HIS
WAY TO FREEDOM.

whose work quickly developed a recognizable stamp of sometimes crude violence, often unpalatable but undeniably compelling.

The central character of *Apache*, Massai, is based on historical fact. A legendary figure of American Indian lore, he refused to join in the surrender of the Apaches under Geronimo in the 1880s. The film follows his flight from his US government pursuers, led by Al Sieber (John McIntire), for whom his capture becomes a personal crusade, and his efforts to live peaceably with his squaw (Jean Peters) on land which he considers to belong by right to his people.

While the black wig and body make-up did little to disguise the Anglo-Saxon movie star beneath, Lancaster's performance was taut, heroic and moving, in a film rare at that time in taking a sympathetic view of the Indians' plight. Massai, as played by Burt, is a figure of dignity and courage, though unafraid to kill when necessary, or to treat his much-loved wife with shocking harshness when he believes (wrongly) that she has betrayed him. Jean Peters, soon to end a short career by marrying the eccentric Howard Hughes, was excellent, although the two stars reportedly did not get on. Aldrich was quoted as finding Lancaster 'not an easy man to get along with, but quite responsive'.

Reviews on both sides of the Atlantic were mixed, with the 'happy' ending coming in for particular criticism. The original ending, in which Massai is shot in the back by his pursuers, was in fact re-filmed in response to the pleas of distributors and exhibitors, who felt that audiences would be alienated if the star were allowed to die. Hecht and Lancaster capitulated with some reluctance and, many years later, Burt told an audience at the National Film Theatre in London, 'I must say that though I hated the idea I went along with them and the picture was very successful, so I will never know how the other ending would have been. As I have done many times in my life, I sold my soul to the Devil.'

The film, shot in widescreen and Technicolor with a budget of a million dollars, was an instant and hefty success, grossing $3 million on its first release in 1954, a figure that doubled in due course, and Hecht-Lancaster retained Aldrich for another Western to follow immediately on *Apache*.

Released towards the close of 1954, *Vera Cruz* co-starred Burt with a revered veteran of the screen and saddle, Gary Cooper. (Lancaster had originally wanted Cary Grant for Cooper's role, but Grant, the only major male star of his generation never to make a Western, would not be persuaded.)

Filmed on location in Mexico, *Vera Cruz* concerned two loners, each a sharpshooting adventurer on the make during the Mexican revolution. They hire themselves out to the Emperor Maximilian as escorts to a wagon train carrying a glamorous countess (Denise Darcel) and a large

THE POLISHED TRANE (GARY COOPER) AND THE UNCOUTH ERIN (LANCASTER), OBSERVED BY THE EMPEROR'S AIDE (HENRY BRANDON) AT THE MEXICAN COURT IN *VERA CRUZ*.

cache of gold to the coast. In the course of the often violent action, the plot becomes a complex web of cross and double-cross, with the protagonists out to filch the gold for themselves until Cooper, signalled as a good guy from the start, decides that the proper place for the treasure is with the rebels and shoots it out with the dissenting Lancaster.

The movie marked the first time that Burt played a dyed-in-the-wool villain – clothed from head to foot in black lest anyone should miss the point. Joe Erin (Lancaster) is a shoddy, amoral character and, despite a lot of the Lancaster grin and an air of energetic, macho bonhomie, he comes across as thoroughly unlikeable. Deferring to Cooper as both a character and an actor, Lancaster comes off badly, his extrovert over-playing emphasized by the languid, laconic, seen-it-all-before Cooper. Aldrich directed with gusto, but with an ugly, disturbing edge both to the gunplay and to Erin's relationship with the countess, and the respectable critics were unimpressed. Crowther in the *New York Times* considered it 'a pretty atrocious film' and Lancaster 'a mess as a villain who displays his meanness by frequent diabolic laughs'. It is difficult to disagree, though Britain's *Monthly Film Bulletin* thought Burt's performance 'subtle and attractive'. The public flocked, and it was another hit for Hecht-Lancaster and UA, eventually amassing some $11 million against its production cost of $1.6 million.

In 1955, a few months after the release of *Vera Cruz*, an article appeared in *Confidential* magazine, a virulent publication that peddled scandalous 'revelations'. The piece alleged that Lancaster's brutal treatment of Denise Darcel in *Vera Cruz* was not a million miles away from his off-screen behaviour, and that he was known to abuse women. It was one of the rare occasions on which rumours about the star were published, but they

Burt's marriage had suffered severely from his long and passionate involvement with Shelley Winters.

remained unsubstantiated and were rightly ignored by the subject of the accusations. Burt's marriage had suffered severely from his long and passionate involvement with actress Shelley Winters, casual affairs, and the worry of his son William having contracted polio at the age of three (he eventually recovered fully). None the less, Norma had given birth to their third daughter, Sighle-Ann (pronounced Sheila), in July 1954.

The gutter press and the film critics notwithstanding, Burt had delivered two consecutive box-office successes and was ready to embark on the directing career which had long been his professed aim and object.

His choice of material brought the third Western in a row from

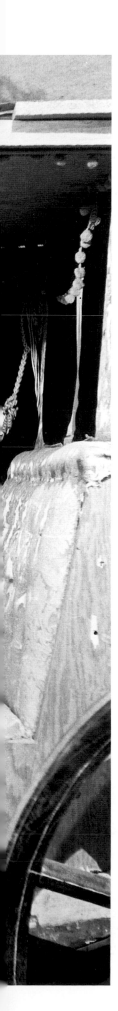

Hecht-Lancaster, though one of a different hue from its predecessors. Adapted from *The Gabriel Horn*, a novel by Felix Holt, *The Kentuckian* is an old-fashioned tale of frontier life and aspirations — a character-driven piece that reflects life in the more settled communities of the West.

The story concerns Big Eli, an idealistic but naive and uneducated widower who, with his small son, sets off in pursuit of a new life in Texas, where land and opportunity are in generous supply. Journeying first to the town where his brother is a prosperous merchant, Eli uses his savings to buy out Hannah (Dianne Foster), a cruelly treated indentured serving maid, and is sidetracked into remaining with his brother's family and joining the business. He falls foul of the sadistic town bully (Walter Matthau, making his screen debut), and deludes himself into a romance with the local schoolteacher (Diana Lynn), before finally realizing that his real destiny lies in going to Texas with Small Eli and his true love, Hannah.

ABOVE: TRANE, ERIN, THE COUNTESS (DENISE DARCEL) – AND THE BOX OF GOLD THAT ALL THREE WANT.
LEFT: BURT AND DENISE DARCEL SHARE A JOKE ON SET WITH DIRECTOR ROBERT ALDRICH.

The film is not altogether uninteresting, and the direction reflects that sensitivity of perception that was so often the keynote of Lancaster's best acting. It is, however, too long, too slow, too ponderous and, at its core, unconvincing. It was certainly ambitious in scale for a first-time director, though Lancaster doubtless believed that he had been in enough movies to know how it was done. The one really gripping sequence in the film, alive with action and tension, comes when he defends himself with his bare hands against Matthau wielding a bull-whip.

During the filming, in addition to being on screen in virtually every take, Lancaster displayed his now well-known and ruthless drive for perfection, but the results of his labours brought a bitterly disappointing critical thumbs-down. The *New York Times* felt that the film ran 'wild in mood and tempo with no sense of dramatic focus or control', and *Variety* thought it 'a bit too self-conscious, as though the director and the actor couldn't quite agree'. The movie failed to generate much excitement or indeed revenue at the box office, but the astute critic C.A. Lejeune, writing in the London *Observer*, discussed *The Kentuckian* in relation to John Ford's *The Wagonmaster*, which was enjoying a revival during the same week. She said, 'As a manipulator of material, Mr Lancaster stands to Mr Ford in much the relation of a kindergarten pupil to a professor. The one knows next to nothing of the controlled flow of visual imagery of which the other has been a master for more than thirty years. He is still comparatively artless, but he is learning... I think he must also be a man with an untaught love for the fine and imaginative thing.' The film itself she felt to be 'a rough buckskin type of film with a glint of poetry here and there, and plenty of clean air blowing through'. And the critic for the *Monthly Film Bulletin* perhaps got to the heart of the enterprise in suggesting that the film, with its 'romantic insistence on the virtues of the noble savage... reflects a personality'.

'...the hardest job of my life... But it's the best job in pictures because when you're a director, you are God.'

Lancaster had much to say about the experience. 'I actually found it the hardest job of my life... Nobody works harder than the director if he's at all serious. His work is never finished, simply never finished... But it's the best job in pictures because when you're a director, you are God. And, you know, that's the best job in town.'

The statement is artless and revealing, and it is interesting that his first-hand knowledge of a director's burdens did little to quell his

DRESSED FOR HIS ROLE AS BIG ELI IN *THE KENTUCKIAN*, ACTOR-DIRECTOR LANCASTER REHEARSES DONALD MACDONALD, WHO PLAYED HIS SON, LITTLE ELI.

interference and irascibility on other men's pictures for some years to come. He put the failure of *The Kentuckian* down to flaws in the screenplay of which, he claimed, he and his writer A.B. Guthrie were always aware, always attempting to eliminate, but never quite succeeding. He also voiced the belief that 'I will probably never again act in a picture I also direct. Much as I've enjoyed working as an actor in the past, it's possible I may quit that phase of showbusiness and concentrate on being a director. That's been my real ambition ever since starring in motion pictures.'

He had indeed been vociferous in this vein from the outset, and frequently returned to the theme. As late as 1973 he told the National Film Theatre audience, 'I am going to go into the field of direction a little more. I feel I'm at an age now – although I won't stop acting – I should begin to do things that I really want… I'd like to sit back and find

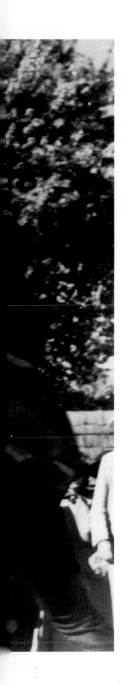

something and shape it. But fate has dealt me a terrible blow. It's made a movie star out of me and I'm caught in my own trap.' It was a trap in which he remained for the rest of his life. Other than a co-directing venture in 1974, *The Kentuckian* remained his only directorial credit.

The award-winning playwright Paddy Chayefsky was a linchpin of the golden age of American television drama. He excelled in realistic dramas that focused on the lives of ordinary people, of which his TV play *Marty* was the paradigm. It tells the story of a plug-ugly, lonely Bronx butcher and a plain, mousy, equally lonely schoolteacher who find love together. On paper, it was not the kind of subject apparently likely to set the box office alight, but Harold and Burt recognized its potential. Hecht's drive and efficiency as a producer, together with his partner's commitment and determination, brought the project to fruition, with the original TV director Delbert Mann, a screen adaptation by Chayefsky, and two relative unknowns, Ernest Borgnine and Betsy Blair, starring.

A favourite of movie lovers, *Marty* is a testament to Burt's stated willingness to take risks in the interests of quality.

Although United Artists liked the script, they viewed it as art-house fare. Made for only $330,000, the film premièred at the Sutton Theatre in New York, a small venue specializing in foreign and minority-taste movies, before releasing nationally in medium-sized venues willing to give it an extended run in the hope of attracting audiences through word of mouth. In the event, *Marty* returned an eventual gross of over $4 million on its original investment, was voted best picture at the 1955 Cannes Festival and, at Oscar time, won Best Picture, Best Screenplay, Best Director and Best Actor, the latter making a star of Borgnine. Forty years later, *Marty* remains a favourite of movie lovers (it is the subject of the climactic question in Robert Redford's 1993 *Quiz Show*) and is a testament to Burt's stated willingness to take risks in the interests of quality. The results were a matter for rejoicing for the partners and for UA, whose costly association with their producer-star was paying dividends way beyond the failure of *The Kentuckian*.

There was one more movie to deliver under the current UA deal, but before making *Trapeze*, Burt returned to Hal Wallis to co-star with the volcanic and magnificent Italian actress Anna Magnani in *The Rose Tattoo*. Tennessee Williams' play, characteristically set in the steamy South, is the tale of the passionate widow of a sexually magnetic husband, whose life is going to rack and ruin through her obsession with the dead man's

memory, particularly when she learns that he was faithless. After much resistance, she succumbs to the charms of a reckless, happy-go-lucky, somewhat dim-witted but lusty truck driver (Lancaster) who reminds her of her husband and whose devotion brings her back to life, at the same time freeing her daughter (Marisa Pavan) from the shackles of her mother's anti-male bitterness and disillusion.

Williams originally wrote the play for Magnani, but her English was then insufficiently fluent to sustain a Broadway stage performance and Maureen Stapleton played the role, opposite Eli Wallach. The playwright agreed to the film on condition that he write the screenplay adaptation himself and that Magnani would star. As with *Come Back, Little Sheba*, *The Rose Tattoo* is unequivocally a star vehicle for the lead actress, but Lancaster once again identified both the challenge and the possible glory of taking second place.

The film, made on location in Key West, was in the hands of Daniel Mann, who had directed *Sheba*, and the material was once again uncommercial. Lancaster came to rank Magnani – as he had Shirley Booth – as the most exceptional actress he had ever worked with while, according

LEFT: IN EARNEST DISCUSSION WITH ITALIAN FIREBRAND ANNA MAGNANI, THE LEADING LADY IMPORTED FOR *THE ROSE TATTOO*. RIGHT: THE ACTORS' CONCENTRATION AND COMMITMENT IS PALPABLE AS THEY WORK TOGETHER ON THEIR RESPECTIVE ROLES.

to Hal Wallis, 'Magnani fell head over heels for her co-star. He was just her type of big, broad-shouldered he-man. But he wasn't attracted to her and she got nowhere and gallantly settled for friendship. Though they both had enormous egos, they were unselfish in their playing and respected each other's talents.'

When the film was released (by Paramount) in late 1955, the critics were justifiably fulsome in their praise for Magnani, an actress then known only to those followers of the Italian cinema who had marvelled at Roberto Rossellini's *Rome – Open City*, in which she had starred. Not conventionally beautiful, she was a magnetic personality and a brilliant actress whom director William Dieterle called 'the last of the great shameless emotionalists', and Jean Renoir 'probably the greatest actress I have ever worked with'. As anyone who sees *The Rose Tattoo* can testify, these descriptions are no exaggeration, and when the Oscars rolled around, Magnani duly carried off the Best Actress trophy. Also nominated as Best Picture, the film lost to Hecht-Lancaster's *Marty*, so, one way and another, Lancaster was riding high.

The actor's reviews for *The Rose Tattoo* were mixed. *Variety* found him 'over his head and overboard as a moron whose brawn attracts Miss Magnani'. The *New York Times* was favourable, and the *New Yorker* thought he 'wasn't bad as the dim-witted suitor'. But the notice that perhaps most accurately summed up an undeniably honourable effort, in which Lancaster displayed moments of great sweetness amid the rambunctious

Filmed in the Cirque d'Hiver, *Trapeze* is a stunt-filled acrobatic extravaganza redolent with the smell of the sawdust.

extroversion of his performance, was that of Arthur Knight in the *Saturday Review*, who wrote, 'He attacks the part with zest and intelligence... But one is always aware that he is acting, that he is playing a part that fits him physically but is beyond his emotional depth. His strong-toothed grin, his cropped, slicked-back hair, his bent-kneed walk are, like his precarious Italian accent, mannerisms and devices carefully acquired for the occasion and barely more than skin deep. The earnestness of his effort only serves to highlight Magnani's own complete submergence in her role.'

Lancaster's next role was the first fully to utilize his circus background. Adapted from Max Catto's novel *The Killing Frost*, directed by England's Carol Reed, and co-starring Tony Curtis and the Italian beauty Gina Lollobrigida, *Trapeze* was the last – and the most profitable – of the five films due to United Artists from Hecht-Lancaster.

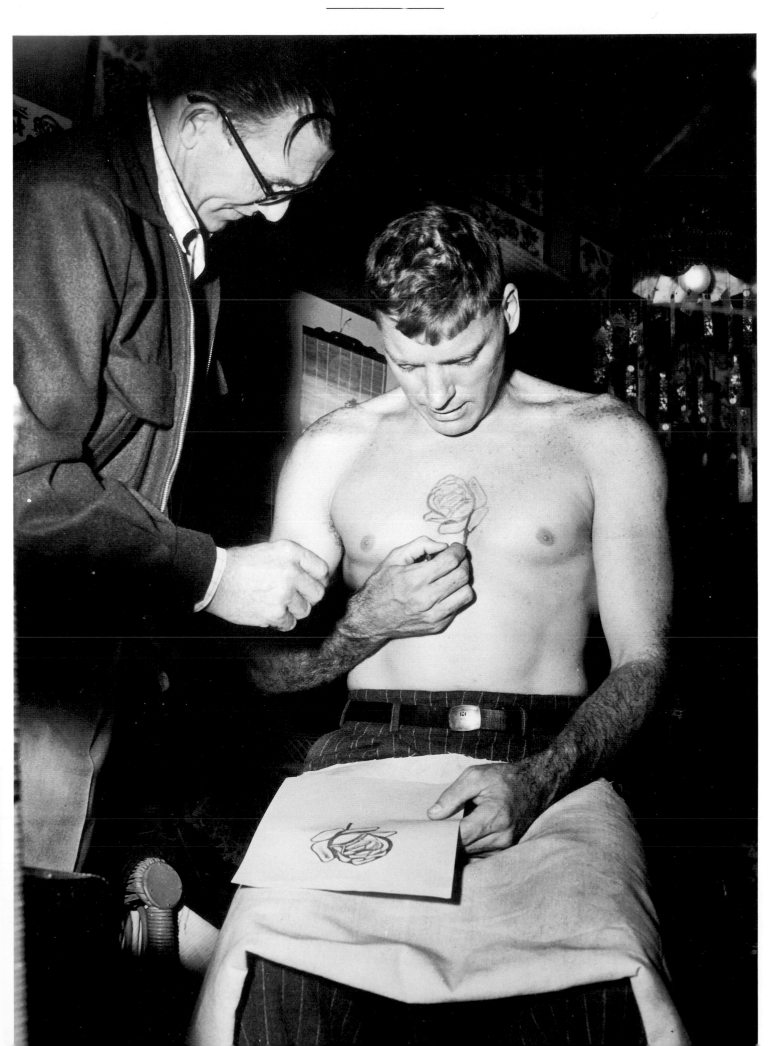

Filmed on location in the famous Cirque d'Hiver in Paris, *Trapeze* is a stunt-filled acrobatic extravaganza redolent with the smell of the saw-dust. In truth, it is more melodrama than drama, but it none the less generates real tension despite the lack of in-depth characterization in the screenplay and a heavily contrived love triangle.

Lancaster played Mike Gribble, formerly a trapeze artist famed for performing the nigh-impossible triple somersault until he mistimed it, resulting in injury and a permanent limp. Embittered, and his nerve gone, he is working as an aerial rigger when he is approached by Orsini (Curtis), a young acrobat arrived from America to seek his help in learning to perform the triple. After the predictable scenes of refusal, Gribble acquiesces, trains the young man and becomes his catcher. Things go awry when an ambitious female aerialist (Lollobrigida) muscles in on the act, playing the two men off against each other.

IN THE CIRCUS DRAMA *TRAPEZE*, OLD HAND BURT PLAYED OLD HAND MIKE GRIBBLE, TRAINING AMBITIOUS NOVICE TINO ORSINI (TONY CURTIS, RIGHT).

For all its soap operatics, *Trapeze* works — partly because the major focus is on the acrobatics, partly because the star, ably supported by Curtis, gives a complete, convincing and rounded performance, free of histrionics or superficial 'character' acting. Gribble's inner torments, as conveyed by Burt, are truthful and moving, and when he takes to the wire again, clad in glamorous circus white, it is clear that, at almost forty-three, he was still a magnificent physical specimen. His personal self-discipline was unassailable: a controlled healthy diet, continuing work-outs with Nick Cravat, and regular running to keep in shape, all of which no doubt contributed to counteracting the effects of his heavy smoking. For *Trapeze* he did the majority of his aerial stunts himself, but employed Eddie Ward of the Ringling Brothers Circus as technical adviser and double for the most dangerous moments. He had worked with Ward in the Gorman Brothers Circus in 1935 and trusted him implicitly.

On its release in 1956, the film was praised for its action and atmosphere and was a clear commercial hit, returning some $18 million to the coffers of Hecht-Lancaster and a delighted United Artists. As Tino Balio puts it in his book on United Artists, 'A remarkable string of hits had catapulted Hecht-Lancaster into the forefront of the independent ranks in Hollywood. The company's reputation rested on a group of solid commercial action pictures, but *Marty* added an extra dimension. Hecht-Lancaster had demonstrated to the trade not only the durability of Lancaster's appeal as a star but also an uncanny knack for starting trends.'

Much credit for this must go to Harold Hecht, a highly intelligent man and a first-class producer, with superb business acumen. He was the antithesis of Lancaster in every way — small, dark, Jewish and earnest, he felt overshadowed by Burt's golden glamour and resented his partner's joky habit of referring to him as 'Lord Gnome'. For his part,

'HE FLIES THROUGH THE AIR WITH THE GREATEST OF EASE...' BURT, AT FORTY-THREE, WAS AS PHYSICALLY FIT AS EVER AND STILL ABLE TO PERFORM HIS OWN ACROBATICS.

Lancaster was unstinting in his admiration of Hecht's professional skills, but felt he lacked imagination and was too concerned with commercially viable material. Despite the success they had made of their joint venture, their growing differences in taste and approach were placing an increasing strain on their relationship, and their chief story consultant, James Hill, an affable, even-tempered man, found himself serving as a buffer between them.

The United Artists contract had run its course and the company had to consider whither next. They decided to stay with UA, where Lew Wasserman drove a hard bargain that left Arthur Krim and company reeling at the concessions they had allowed themselves to make. Suffice to say that the new contract was worth a great deal of money. James Hill became a partner and the company once again changed its name to become Hecht-Hill-Lancaster, increasing its staff and announcing a proposed schedule of six pictures a year. As Balio sums it up, 'With offices in Beverly Hills and New York — the former acting as a production headquarters and the latter as a story department — and a permanent staff of thirty-eight employees, Hecht-Lancaster now had the look of a Hollywood major, *sans* studio. Overhead to maintain this operation came to $300,000 a year.'

In addition to this extraordinary expansion, the company became the first independent outfit to open its own publicity offices in Europe and the Far East, and planned two parallel production programmes — one tailored for Burt, the other to bring in outside filmmakers. It was indeed starting to look like a fully-fledged movie studio, with Burt now a curious hybrid: popular star on the one hand, mini-mogul on the other. But for all his passionate involvement and determined say in the artistic and business affairs of Hecht-Hill-Lancaster, it was ultimately the actor, the egoist and the man who wanted to see money in the bank that prevailed in his career choices.

Burt ended his ten-year relationship with Hal Wallis on a characteristic note, trading off a film he didn't want to do for one that he did, and once again it was the maligned producer's choice that proved the more successful. The actor had an outstanding two-film commitment to Wallis which the latter asked him to fulfil by playing Marshal Wyatt Earp in *Gunfight at the OK Corral* opposite his old stablemate Kirk

LEFT: THE GRAND FINALE AT THE
CIRQUE D'HIVER: BURT, GINA
LOLLOBRIGIDA AND TONY CURTIS.
ABOVE: THE HECHT-LANCASTER
OUTPUT WAS MOUNTING STEADILY.

Douglas' Doc Holliday, but, for reasons that are unclear, Burt was resistant to the proposal. Meanwhile, Wallis had bought the film rights to N. Richard Nash's play *The Rainmaker*. He planned to star Katharine Hepburn as Lizzie, a repressed, self-deprecating Kansas spinster revitalized by the arrival of a spirited con man who promises to bring rain to her family's parched farmland while reawakening her barren soul with flattery and the gift of confidence.

The role of Starbuck, the itinerant peddler of patent elixirs, certainly seemed tailor-made for Lancaster's powerful presence and there can be little doubt that the idea of co-starring with Hepburn, the long-running aristocrat of the American screen, must have been irresistible. As Wallis told it, 'Burt telephoned me in the middle of the night to say that if I would let him play Starbuck, the lead in *The Rainmaker*, he would do *Gunfight at the OK Corral*, and that would take care of our two remaining commitments. I agreed and they were two of Burt's best pictures.'

Whether *The Rainmaker* can be considered one of Burt's 'best pictures' remains open to argument, but there were, and are, those who appreciated the whimsical parable (as Starbuck rides away, having conned a hundred dollars out of Lizzie's family, the rain indeed comes down) and one of the most curious screen pairings of the decade. The legion of Hepburn's fans thought her marvellous as a Midwest farm girl heading for the shelf and finally realizing that happiness lies with her diffident suitor (Wendell Corey); and Burt's admirers appreciated the undeniable charm and sincerity that is detectable in his somewhat posturing and over-the-top performance.

Top billing was given to Lancaster. Despite *The African Queen* (1951) and *Summertime* (1955), Hepburn's Hollywood forays were now sporadic, and she no longer had the drawing power of her earlier career. The Massachusetts blue-blood and the East Harlem street kid got off to a bad start — Burt was late on set on the first day of filming and the outspoken Hepburn let rip at him on the subject of manners and professionalism. It never happened again, but then it had not happened before. In such matters, Burt's own professional discipline was normally faultless. Their personal relationship continued warily although they got along well enough. Lancaster was a breed of actor far removed from his leading lady's school of experience, and she was reported as being out of sympathy with his approach. What he felt about her we are left to guess.

The end result is uneven, but *The Rainmaker*, directed by Joseph Anthony and released at the end of 1956, proved successful and the critics were generally kind. *Variety* got it right when they called Lancaster 'colorful' and 'ingratiating'; Britain's distinguished critic Dilys Powell, who, over the years, had been very fair to the actor, accorded both brickbats and bouquets as appropriate when she wrote, 'The glib visitor is played by Burt Lancaster. His gestures and poses are a shade athletic, and once or twice I had the fancy that he was still impersonating the Crimson Pirate. He is saddled too, with awkward stretches of dialogue, fake-imaginative phrases which, however well they may accord with the character on stage, on the screen make one restive. But when it is needed, he brings a hint of uncertainty to the part and the result is a very likeable pathos.'

JOY FOR THE RAMBUNCTIOUS STARBUCK AS HIS PROMISED RAIN FINALLY FALLS.

While Burt was filming *The Rainmaker*, the production arm of Hecht-Hill-Lancaster was busy with its first film under the new UA contract. Again written by Paddy Chayefsky and directed by Delbert Mann, and again with a cast of relative unknowns, headed by Don Murray, *The Bachelor Party* was another small-scale film with which the producers hoped to repeat the success of *Marty*. However, although it was critically appreciated, its downbeat subject failed to attract audiences, despite an Academy Award nomination for Carolyn Jones. Financially, the movie was a complete failure, and Hecht-Hill-Lancaster ended up owing UA a substantial sum under the complex terms of their contract.

On 26 October 1881, at Tombstone, Arizona, a shoot-out occurred at the OK Corral between the members of the Clanton family on one side, and US Marshal Wyatt Earp, a couple of his brothers, and the hard-drinking, consumptive gambler Doc Holliday on the other. So much is part of the Old West's less than savoury history. Earp, Holliday and the Clantons, however, came to pass into the mythology of the West, and became a favourite topic for filmmakers over a number of years, the best-loved and most haunting version being John Ford's *My Darling Clementine* (1946), with Henry Fonda and Victor Mature.

Gunfight at the OK Corral was, and is, a much-lauded Western of the period, well summed up by the *New York Herald Tribune*: 'No single event in the movie will surprise anybody, but everything is done with an extra degree of quality.' Directed with strength and clarity by John Sturges, who would tackle the subject of *Gunfight* again in *Hour of the Gun* in 1967, the film was scripted by Leon Uris and strongly cast with a line-up that included Lee Van Cleef, John Ireland (as the Ringo Kid) and the young Dennis Hopper as Billy Clanton. Rhonda Fleming played the glamorous and entirely fictitious love interest invented for Earp, while the splendid Jo Van Fleet gave a brave and convincing performance as the alcoholic whore who loves Holliday, a character dimly based on truth.

The movie was shot on location in Arizona, and the sparks flew. A much-repeated story recounts how Lancaster reduced Douglas almost to tears by humiliating him in front of a group of autograph hunters. Surrounded by these fans, Burt said, 'Why don't you ask Mr Douglas for his? Great performer. Of course, you don't recognize him without his built-up shoes.' Columnist Sheilah Graham had dubbed the two stars the 'Terrible Tempered Twins', and wrote that 'Burt was autocratic

'Burt was autocratic from the start. Kirk waited three years and seven films before he dared to be himself.'

from the start. Kirk waited three years and seven films before he dared to be himself.' Despite this clash of two monumental egos and Burt's cruel propensity to needle his co-star, it was during this time that the pair cemented the friend-ship that would temper their rivalry.

Director Sturges coped admirably with the actors' com-bined efforts to run the show. As Wallis recounted it, 'From the start, both stars asserted them-

RESPECTFUL ADVERSARIES: DOC HOLLIDAY (KIRK DOUGLAS) AND WYATT EARP (LANCASTER) IN *GUNFIGHT AT THE OK CORRAL*.

selves. They reminded us constantly that they were directors as well as actors and tried to override Sturges, but John was a match for them. They rewrote their dialogue at night, but this was an exercise in futility, as I insisted that the lines be read exactly as Leon Uris had written them. Burt finally exploded, demanding that John let him play a scene his way, with dialogue he had written. It was totally unrelated to the action, but John humoured him. Burt played the scene to the hilt, shouting himself hoarse. The speech was out of his system. The film was also out of the camera.'

Contrary to what might have been expected, the finished product was an engrossing Western in which Lancaster's earnest, almost noble marshal, attempting to uphold virtue in the face of vice, is an authorita-tive and attractive figure. He was eminently well suited to the role as written and directed, and, though metaphorically outgunned by Kirk Douglas' portrayal of the far more flamboyant and gritty Doc Holliday, he emerged as a fully-fledged Western hero, his public image enhanced.

The film cost Wallis a fortune in salaries to Lancaster and Douglas – things had changed a lot since he nurtured them as young actors on min-imal wages in *I Walk Alone* – but the investment proved a sound one.

Thus Lancaster ended his association with Wallis on a mutually benefi-cial note. He returned to Los Angeles and his opulent executive office at Hecht-Hill-Lancaster, ready to widen his horizons and expand his achievements still further. Despite intimations that a new crop of young, handsome and talented actors, Paul Newman and Brando among them, would soon be snapping at his heels, in 1957 Burt Lancaster was still a huge star. And, most significantly, he was now a major power player in Hollywood.

A FRIENDLY CHAT? BURT GAVE KIRK A HARD TIME DURING FILMING, BUT THEY NONE THE LESS CEMENTED WHAT WOULD PROVE A LIFELONG RELATIONSHIP.

Sweet smell of *SUCCESS*

CHAPTER FIVE

'It was the greatest failure our company ever made. We lost a fortune on it, but it has become a critic's darling over the years. Not enough moviegoers cared for it. I don't think they understood the background, the rather strange Clifford Odets dialogue.'

Thus said Lancaster of the first film in which he starred for his own company and UA under the second leg of their contract. Today *Sweet Smell of Success* is classed as Hecht-Hill-Lancaster at its best, and Burt's performance as the pathologically venomous New York syndicated newspaper columnist J.J. Hunsecker is considered one of his most memorable. The film enjoys critical approval and a wide following

Sweet Smell of Success inhabits the heart of a moral sewer in which greed and amorality power ambition.

whenever and wherever it is shown but, at the time, although its quality was critically recognized, the public was notable by its absence and the film incurred a large debt for the company.

The material was Burt's own choice, against the wishes of Harold Hecht, who strongly and steadfastly disliked both the subject and the finished product. The actor commissioned Ernest Lehman to adapt his own novella, then brought in the distinguished playwright Clifford (*The Big Knife*) Odets to work on it, thus achieving a superior level of literacy and originality in the hard-hitting dialogue – and fighting with Odets along the way.

The film inhabits the heart of a moral sewer in which greed and amorality power ambition. The malevolent Hunsecker, a maker and breaker of lives and reputations, has one love – his younger sister (Susan Harrison), to whom his devotion is unhealthily obsessive. He hires an equally amoral publicist, Sidney Falco (Tony Curtis), to break up her relationship with a musician by framing the latter as a Communist and a

As the travelling salesman-turned-evangelist in Richard Brooks' *Elmer Gantry* (1960).

ABOVE: WITH DIRECTOR ALEXANDER MACKENDRICK DURING THE FILMING OF *SWEET SMELL OF SUCCESS*. THE FILM BROUGHT A NEW CHALLENGE FOR LANCASTER, AND ONE TO WHICH HE ROSE MAGNIFICENTLY.
RIGHT: AS THE VENOMOUS J.J. HUNSECKER, DISHING THE DIRT WITH HIS TOADYING SIDEKICK SIDNEY FALCO (TONY CURTIS).

drug addict. *En route* to the denouement, the sleazy and corrupt night world inhabited by the Hunseckers and Falcos is uncompromisingly exposed in an atmospherically photographed (by James Wong Howe) New York, peopled by human reptiles.

Lancaster hired the British director Alexander Mackendrick, best known for films such as the Ealing comedy *Whisky Galore*. It seemed an odd choice, but the result justified Burt's instincts. Getting there, however, was fraught with difficulties. According to Burt, Mackendrick never seemed to know what he wanted.

'He'd set up shots on the soundstage for a scene that would play six minutes... The camera moved continuously – into close-ups, pulling back, shooting over here to this person. Move in, turn. We rehearsed all day, until four in the afternoon, just to get the technical part down. The head grip and the rest of the crew were sweating, knowing that if they missed one mark, the shot would be ruined. But we did it, clicked it all off. Sandy called "Cut. Print." Then he'd stop, waiting. I'd say, "Something the matter Sandy?" "No, it went fine, you all did it fine... let's do one more." So we went through it again. Again, fine. Cut. I was delighted. We had six minutes of film, a good day's work – and done in the most interesting style. But he still wouldn't be satisfied. He'd shake his head and say, "I don't like it, we've got to change it – change everything." '

That Lancaster put up with this is a testament both to the quality of Mackendrick's work and, indeed, to the mellowing of the actor, who acknowledged, 'We respected Sandy; he was a little kooky, but he was good. He did a marvellous job. It wasn't his fault the picture lost money.'

Mackendrick, for his part, had no reservations about Lancaster and came as near perhaps as anyone has in summing up Burt's star quality. 'One of the things he has, that the stars had,' said the director, 'is that he can walk into a room and there is a change in the heartbeat. If you had some instrument you could measure it. It's like having a wild animal there suddenly. It has to do with aggression and potential violence. I think some politicians have it, but no English actor.'

WITH CLARK GABLE IN
RUN SILENT, RUN DEEP,
A SUPERIOR SUBMARINE
ADVENTURE IN WHICH
LANCASTER PROVED WELL
ABLE TO HOLD HIS OWN IN
THE COMPANY OF THE
PREVIOUS GENERATION'S
LEGENDARY MACHO STAR.

Donning spectacles for the first time on screen and playing a character of unalleviated maliciousness, Lancaster was, as *Variety* noted, undertaking 'a remarkable change of pace'. It is a measure of his capabilities, and remained one of his own favourite roles. The major surprise of the film, though, was Tony Curtis, who, as the oily, wheedling, hustling Falco, proved that his abilities far surpassed the 'pretty boy' label he was in danger of acquiring. ('I'd hate to take a bite out of you. You're a cookie full of arsenic,' says Burt's Hunsecker to Tony's Falco in one of the film's bitingly ironic exchanges.) Curtis, Burt said, 'was absolutely marvellous. It's the best thing he's ever done, I think. It should have won him the Academy Award.'

In an obvious bid for commercial success, the company and Burt enlisted the still considerable drawing power of Clark Gable, the great macho star of a previous generation, gave him top billing, and co-starred him with Burt in a war-movie throwback, *Run Silent, Run Deep*. Set in the claustrophobic confines of a submarine, the movie deals with the conflict and animosity, later growing into mutual respect, between a sub captain (Gable), who is given command of a ship, and the chief officer (Lancaster), who was widely expected to hold that position. Gable, whose previous vessel was sunk by the Japanese in the Bongo Straits, is obsessed, against orders, with finding and destroying the enemy ship responsible, and against all odds, achieves his aim, dying in the process.

The offbeat chemistry of the two very different stars was extremely effective and the film, directed by Robert Wise, was an exciting underwater actioner with authentic atmosphere. Wise recalled that the script decisions and filming were dogged by complicated internal tensions and disagreements between the Hecht-Hill-Lancaster partners, causing difficulties for Gable, but the on-screen tension was splendid, moving Bosley Crowther to say that 'A better film about guys in the "silent service" has not been made.'

He appears to have lacked the clear direction which his power, status and money should have allowed him to pursue.

The policy of choosing a popular money-spinner to offset a worthy loss was becoming the hallmark of Burt's approach, but with only partial success. *Run Silent, Run Deep* was relatively well received and well attended, but came nowhere near to recouping the losses incurred by *Sweet Smell of Success*.

None the less, it was in the year of its release, 1958, that Burt stated publicly, 'I am terribly wealthy. I am worth three-and-a-half million

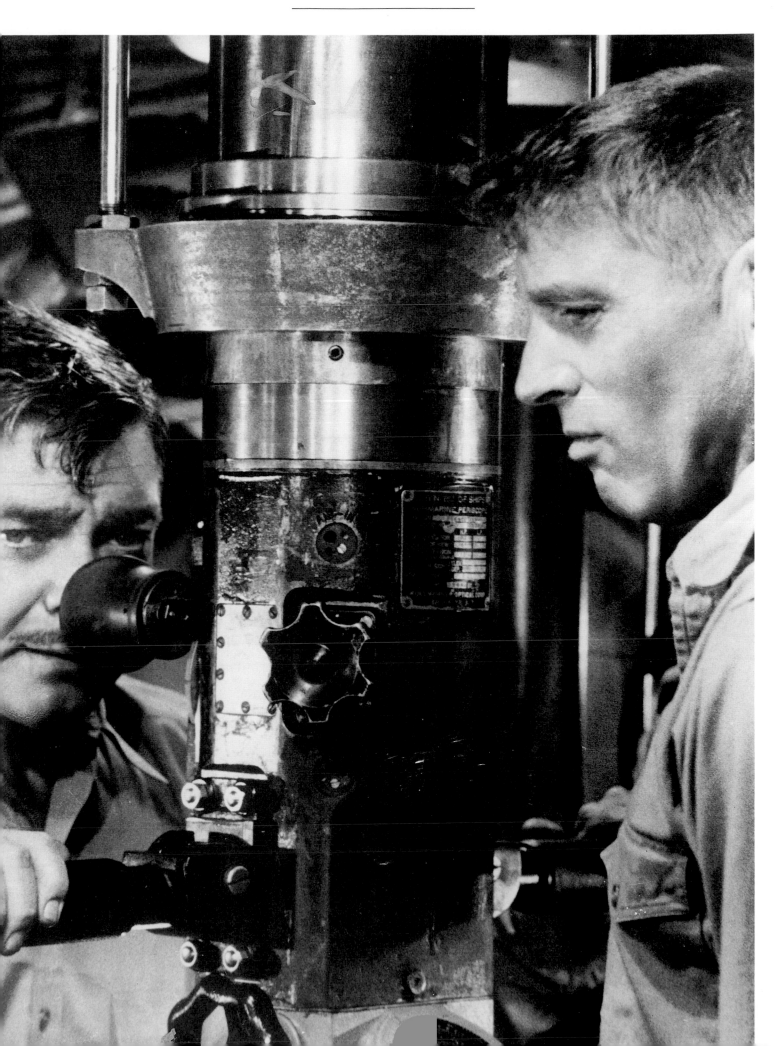

dollars. I have five children. I've got everything I want. What more could I possibly need? I am not moved by the desire to make more money or win more fame. I've got enough of both and there comes a time when you can't get any more of either. I am just interested in doing things that interest me. When I first started in movies I was unsure of myself, and insecure. I would flare up easily. When success comes as quickly as it came to me there are bound to be problems. You ask yourself, "How do I come to be here and have I any right to be here?" It took me a certain amount of time to adjust. Now I think I'm adjusted. I keep calm.'

This self-assessment, with perhaps a hint of self-aggrandizement, and a touch of apology for past offence given, was not a declaration of intent. The enigma of Burt Lancaster appeared as impenetrable as ever. With hindsight, he appears to have lacked the clear direction which his power, status and money should have allowed him to pursue. It is almost impossible to explain the rationale behind some of his choices over the next twenty years, other than to assume that, despite his declared wealth, he needed the money. Certainly, he had five children to support and educate, as well as continuing to take care of his father and employ his elder brother. The company would incur debts to United Artists and, a side of his character not often remarked upon in the ground-swell of criticism, he was discreetly open-handed in his generosity to loyal colleagues and his few valued friends.

For the time being, however, Lancaster's career moves displayed his avowed desire to make, or appear in, worthwhile projects, even if the results too often disappointed.

Terence Rattigan's two-part play *Separate Tables* had enjoyed great success in the West End and on Broadway, with Margaret Leighton and Eric Portman each playing two contrasting roles in a theatrical *tour de force*. Calling the shots for his company, Lancaster bought the screen rights, and the decision was taken to use four stars rather than two. Displaying an eye for real class, Burt hired Laurence Olivier to direct the film, and to star as the tragic, bogus Major Pollock, who befriends the repressed spinster Sybil Railton-Bell (Deborah Kerr), to the chagrin of her bullying mother (Gladys Cooper). Olivier's wife, the beautiful Vivien Leigh, was to play the neurotic estranged wife of John Malcolm, a moody, heavy-drinking writer, who comes to the residential hotel where the action is set in the hope of getting her husband back. He, meanwhile, is involved with the establishment's proprietress (Wendy Hiller).

It was a great line-up that didn't quite see the light of day. Accounts differ as to the reasons for the subsequent falling-out between Olivier and Lancaster, but fall out they did by the beginning of the shoot. Olivier, given that Lancaster not only had cast himself as Malcolm (now made American for credibility), whereas the director had chosen Spencer Tracy, but also was the film's producer, felt he had no option but to resign — and Vivien Leigh with him. She was replaced with the lovely Rita Hayworth, her career on the slide, but married at the time to James Hill. She gave one of her best performances.

The unqualified triumph of the film was David Niven, replacing Olivier with an immaculate and moving performance that justly won him the Best Actor Oscar for 1958. Miss Kerr, her English glamour veiled by steel spectacles, ghastly haircut and shapeless cardigans,

BREAKFASTING AT THEIR SEPARATE TABLES, ALL EYES ARE ON THE DISGRACED MAJOR (DAVID NIVEN). FROM LEFT TO RIGHT, NIVEN, MAY HALLATT, GLADYS COOPER, DEBORAH KERR, CATHLEEN NESBITT, RITA HAYWORTH AND LANCASTER.

Sweet Smell of Success is the one that is admired today, but _Run Silent, Run Deep_ made the money for Hecht-Hill-Lancaster.

TWO FILMS THAT PUT THE NAIL IN THE COFFIN OF HECHT-HILL-LANCASTER. BOTH, MORE ESPECIALLY *THE DEVIL'S DISCIPLE*, WERE ARTISTIC AND COMMERCIAL FAILURES.

earned her fourth Academy nomination, and Wendy Hiller won the Oscar for Best Supporting Actress.

Though the introduction of two Americans into the setting seems a little odd, the story — adapted by Rattigan himself with John Gay — remains a quintessentially English character study, delving into the tragedies of ordinary lives. The film was critically well received, with *Variety* congratulating Hecht-Hill-Lancaster on 'undertaking a story that does not meet the conception of what is generally considered sure-fire material in today's market'. But in the light of their assertion that 'it has the ingredients to interest and draw the more discriminating filmgoer', box-office receipts served only to demonstrate that discriminating film-goers, then as now, were in the minority.

Admirably undaunted, Lancaster continued on his singular way, but this time the result was an unmitigated disaster. He joined forces with Kirk Douglas' Bryna productions to make George Bernard Shaw's *The Devil's Disciple* on location in England, with Alexander Mackendrick directing. This tale of how the British came to lose their American colonies in the War of Independence was originally planned as a $3 million colour film, of which a massive $600,000 went to the Shaw Estate for the rights. The project had run into script problems and was shelved for a time until Douglas expressed interest, and it went ahead on half the intended budget, shot in black and white. This time, Mackendrick's time- and money-consuming methods could not be accommodated, and he was replaced by Guy Hamilton halfway through. Lancaster and Douglas co-starred as, respectively, the puritanical pacifist man of the cloth, Anthony Anderson, and the scoundrelly Dick Dudgeon. With any bitterness over *Separate Tables* put to one side, Laurence Olivier played the British general, Burgoyne, and was acknowledged as the only saving grace of a picture that emerged as a stylistic hodge-podge that did nothing for either the careers or the coffers of its joint producer-stars. Nobody went to see it, and it was the nail in the coffin of the Hecht-Hill-Lancaster marriage with UA.

SLIGHTLY STRAINED SMILES FROM JANETTE SCOTT, KIRK DOUGLAS, LANCASTER AND LAURENCE OLIVIER DURING THE MAKING OF *THE DEVIL'S DISCIPLE* ON LOCATION IN ENGLAND.

Hecht had, meanwhile, proceeded with other productions under the independent filmmaking arm of the company, which had made four interesting small-scale movies during 1959. These included *Take a Giant Step*, about a black kid's life in a middle-class New England town; and *Summer of the Seventeenth Doll* (released in 1960), adapted from Ray Lawler's Australian play and made on location in that country with Ernest Borgnine starring. None of the pictures made money and, finally, at the end of 1959, United Artists forced Hecht-Hill-Lancaster to retrench their operations.

As Ben Zachary in The Unforgiven, with co-star Audrey Hepburn.

Payments for overheads from UA to the company were dramatically sliced from $5,000 to $1,500 a week, resulting in the closure of H-H-L's London and New York offices, and a major staff cutback. The company owed UA almost $4 million in accumulated deficits on their string of money-losers. Complex negotiations for settlement of debts to UA dragged on with Harold Hecht until 1966, but Lancaster's share of the liabilities was settled in 1964, with the studio buying out his interest in the earlier Hecht-Lancaster movies. However, this was not the end of the actor's association with the studio. Arthur Krim wrote to him, 'I just want you to know that whether it be as producer, director, or star, or a combination of any two or more of the capacities, we would like to keep doing pictures with you for many years to come.' This proved to be the case and, under the aegis of UA, Lancaster gave some of his finest performances.

Meanwhile, still under the H-H-L banner, with James Hill as producer – after which he parted from the company – Burt went to Durango in Mexico to make a Western for John Huston, in which he co-starred with the enchanting but badly miscast Audrey Hepburn. The venture was misguided from the beginning: Ben Maddow's script for *The Unforgiven*, dealing in intolerance and violence between Kiowa Indians and white settlers, appealed to Huston as a serious subject on the theme of racial intolerance, but Hecht-Hill-Lancaster had other ideas, wanting to make it into a blood-and-thunder actioner with maximum box-office

appeal. The violent disagreements that surfaced came too late for Huston to abandon the unhappy project, during the making of which Hepburn sustained a serious fall from a horse which led to her hospitalization, and Audie Murphy nearly drowned during a duck-shooting expedition.

Filmed in harsh conditions in late 1959, the film was not released until several months into the following year, when it received a mixed response. The idea that the ravishing Audrey, playing Burt's adopted sister, turns out to be a Kiowa Indian (paving the way for an after-the-final-fade romance) was frankly risible and, notwithstanding the best efforts of an excellent cast that included Charles Bickford and the estimable Lillian Gish, the picture was not a success. Huston himself stated, 'Some of my pictures I don't care for, but *The Unforgiven* is the only one I actually dislike.'

Lancaster, however, had no time for regrets. Back in the mid-forties Richard Brooks had first asked Burt whether he had read Sinclair Lewis' novel *Elmer Gantry*, a sprawling, powerful tale about a defrocked priest who becomes a corrupt evangelist, and which, in its attack on religious charlatanism and bigotry, had caused much controversy in Christian revivalist circles.

To make the novel into a film had been an *idée fixe* for Brooks for fifteen years and he never wavered in his view that Lancaster was the right man for the title role. Over the years, the two men would bump into each other and on each occasion Brooks would refer to his intended

A CONFRONTATION AT THE CORRAL BETWEEN BEN AND HIS HORSE-LOVING 'SISTER' RACHEL. HEPBURN WAS THROWN FROM A HORSE DURING FILMING, SUFFERING SEVERE INJURIES AND A MISCARRIAGE.

project, for which there was no screenplay, while Burt remained a touch sceptical in his response. Finally Brooks, whose directing credits by then included *The Blackboard Jungle* and *Cat on a Hot Tin Roof*, left MGM, where he was working, and went to Europe on a freighter. He stayed away four months, came back with a completed script, and triumphantly sent it to Burt.

It was the beginning of a long haul. According to Lancaster, when he received the script, he 'didn't care for it... We [he and Brooks] got into a violent argument about it. I told him, "If you really want to do this, I'm with you. But don't start the movie with me as a twenty-year-old kid in a seminary. That's not gonna play. Let's start the film later on." For a while he wouldn't talk to me. Then his agent called and we went back together.'

Brooks told Burt to forget about his golf and 'come over to the studio every day and work with me on this script'. As Burt recalled, 'For seven months we did that. But everything — that, and the preparation — was worth it. It was a labour of love.'

The major studios were not prepared to back a film whose essence was a broadside against religion and when UA finally agreed to go with it, they had no studio available. Brooks rented space at Columbia but, just as shooting got under way, the studio received a letter from a Paramount executive, a Baptist by persuasion, urging them to deny Brooks the use of their premises. Columbia executives bowed to the pressure of the rival company and tried to buy Brooks out of his contract, but he and Burt remained obdurate.

In the film version of Lewis' novel, Gantry is a loud, check-suited but silver-tongued travelling salesman, a drinker, an extrovert and a ladies'

The major studios were not prepared to back a film whose essence was a broadside against religion.

man who, in his youth, was expelled from a theological college for seducing the dean's daughter behind the altar. Down on his luck and living an itinerant existence in sleazy hotels, he wanders into a revivalist tent meeting conducted by Sister Sharon Falconer, is attracted to her and, seeing an opportunity for gain, alternately bulldozes and charms his way into her entourage, becoming a fiery preacher and a major attraction. In time, the morally ambiguous fanatic who is Sister Sharon falls for Gantry, and their joint future seems assured until the reappearance of Lulu Baines (Shirley Jones), the girl he long ago seduced. Now a prostitute, she reveals him as a degenerate fraud by means of a frame-up. The 'preacher' turns the tables and wins back his support, but the foundations of his life collapse when a devastating fire breaks out at a major tent meeting, killing Sister Sharon.

The English gamine Jean Simmons, soon to become Mrs Richard Brooks, made a superb job of Sister Sharon, modelling at least the public face of the character on the most famous of female evangelists, Aimee Semple McPherson. Arthur Kennedy excelled as a cynical newspaperman who follows the religious tour, as did Dean Jagger as Sharon's

THE CHARISMATIC ELMER GANTRY PREACHES THE MESSAGE AND BERATES THE SINNERS.

manager. Brooks brought a furious pace and passion to the direction, using a swirling, almost epic visual technique which eminently suited the vulgar, brash, larger-than-life flavour of the film's milieu and its main character.

As Jean Simmons later recalled, the crucially important revival meetings were partly as successful as they were because 'We didn't use Hollywood extras...Richard would bus in these marvellous old people

from Long Beach who would actually *go* to these Baptist meetings. They really knew the songs. And they really believed that they were in one of their own churches.'

A splendid achievement for all concerned, the film was a particular personal triumph for Burt Lancaster, who had a major influence on the screenplay so brilliantly filleted from Lewis' novel. He had felt that 'Sinclair Lewis wrote Elmer Gantry as a caricature; he made him so one-sided and so bad that it was hard to identify with him… With Dick Brooks I felt that an audience had to recognize something human in him. We weren't trying to uglify him, we were merely trying to make him a recognizable, full-blooded human being with common weaknesses and vanities.'

Lancaster won virtually unanimous critical acclaim. *Variety* noted that he 'pulls out all the stops to create a memorable characterization'; A.H. Weiler of the *New York Times* felt that 'He is an Elmer Gantry who would have delighted the cold enquiring eye and crusading soul of Sinclair Lewis'; according to the *Herald Tribune*, 'Lancaster's portrayal may not be the subtlest performance of his career, but it is certainly among the strongest.'

The British critics followed suit, with the ever-acute, hard-to-please Dilys Powell of the *Sunday Times* praising 'a studied and intelligent

ABOVE: THE POSTER'S LEGENDS SUM UP THE MORAL AMBIGUITY OF THE FILM.

LEFT: ELMER IS NOW THE MAIN ATTRACTION – THE SUITS HAVE SHARPENED, THE FERVOUR AND FIRE HAVE GATHERED MOMENTUM.

performance by Burt Lancaster, a performance which never quite forgets the man's insolent, calculating sexuality'.

For the director, Lancaster was 'one of the most professional actors there are. He really knows what goes into making a movie. He's got a good sense of his own character, isn't afraid to let it all come out...'

The star himself viewed the flashy, demagogical Gantry as 'essentially a ham' and in a much-quoted, somewhat glib, appraisal of his own performance, remarked that, 'It was the easiest role I was ever given to play because I was, in essence, playing myself. Some parts you fall into like an old glove. *Elmer* wasn't really acting – that was me.'

Be that as it may, when the 1960 Academy Awards ceremony rolled around, to his second New York Film Critics best actor award Burt Lancaster added the coveted Best Actor Oscar. It was a moment of glory, all the sweeter for his winning against four other heavyweights who had given superlative performances in first-class films: Jack Lemmon (*The Apartment*), Trevor Howard (*Sons and Lovers*), Spencer Tracy (*Inherit the Wind*) and, sweetest of all, Laurence Olivier (*The Entertainer*). Richard Brooks' commitment to the material was honoured by the Best Screenplay Oscar, and Shirley Jones, better known as the antiseptic heroine of musicals such as *Oklahoma!* and *Carousel,* was voted Best Supporting Actress.

With *Elmer Gantry*, Burt had begun what would prove the best decade of his career.

A singular
man

CHAPTER SIX

Lancaster's first film after his triumph with *Elmer Gantry* little indicated that the 1960s would see him reach the peak of his career, confirming that this most singular of actor-producers played by his own rules.

The Young Savages, based on a novel by Evan Hunter, concerned Hank Bell (Lancaster), an ambitious assistant district attorney who has removed himself from his poor origins through education and marriage to a smart wife (Dina Merrill). Seeking the death penalty for three teenage thugs who have murdered a blind Puerto Rican youth, Bell is forced by a series of incidents to shift from his enthusiastic endorsement of this punitive stance towards the accused — one of whom is the son of his former sweetheart. Ironically, this key role was played by Burt's ex-mistress Shelley Winters.

The film carries a message about the consequences of deprivation and racism that was close to Lancaster's most committed personal concerns, and the East Harlem setting was redolent of his own background. The role was well within his range, but the production proved a bumpy ride with little reward.

Burt and Shelley Winters had maintained a wary distance, and their emotions erupted into a screaming match.

Shelley Winters, refused equal billing with her co-star, turned down the part and Lee Grant was cast. An explosive on-set row between Burt and Miss Grant led to the actress walking out in tears and Miss Winters walking in, on her terms. By now, however, she had to rehearse for a forthcoming theatre tour of *Two for the Seesaw*, so Burt had a replica of her set built in an adjoining studio and sent the dialogue director, future filmmaker Sydney Pollack, to work with her.

As always, Shelley Winters was excellent, but this first reunion since the end of her affair with Burt was difficult for both of them. They had

AS ROBERT STROUD, THE *BIRDMAN OF ALCATRAZ*, RELEASED IN 1962. BURT'S MEMORABLY SKILFUL AND MOVING PERFORMANCE MARKED HIS LAST APPEARANCE FOR HECHT-LANCASTER.

maintained a wary distance from each other, and their emotions erupted into a screaming match during the same scene that had seen the last of Lee Grant — a scene in which the characters dig up their shared past.

With the logistical difficulties, the emotional upheavals, and Burt at his most autocratic and ill-tempered, the shoot was no easy matter for John Frankenheimer, a former TV director making his second feature. With his finely tuned feeling for atmosphere, realism and tension, Frankenheimer would soon enter the first rank of commercial filmmakers with such successes as *The Manchurian Candidate* (1962), and he survived the Lancastrian onslaught sufficiently well for *The Young Savages* to initiate a five-picture collaboration with the star. For the rest, despite some powerful sequences filmed on location in New York, the film failed to find an audience.

Hecht-Hill-Lancaster had bought the rights to *Birdman of Alcatraz*, the biography of Robert Stroud, sentenced in 1909 to twelve years for manslaughter. A fight with a prison guard that resulted in the latter's death consigned Stroud to lifelong solitary confinement, and he was still languishing in prison, despite repeated attempts to secure his release, when H-H-L embarked on the film. What made Stroud's tale remarkable was that he became a self-taught expert in bird diseases after nursing a sick sparrow back to health. Moved from Fort Leavenworth prison to Alcatraz, he was then denied his birds by the newly appointed and hostile director of the Federal Bureau of Prisons.

Lancaster threw himself into a study of Stroud. He recalled that he 'read every letter he [Stroud] wrote and even though I never got to meet him, I felt like I knew him intimately, and I felt I had some idea what it was like to spend forty years in solitary confinement.

'Making this film was like preparing an actual case. I felt like a detective or a lawyer. Ever since I made *Brute Force* I have had a strong, almost obsessive concern for the whole problem of penology.'

Refused permission to film in the actual locations by the director of prisons, who had tried to keep the Stroud story out of the headlines, H-H-L constructed replicas of the prisons at great cost, and filming began under the direction of Charles Crichton, a British director whose forte was English comedy. After three weeks of violent disagreement between the two men, Crichton was fired and John Frankenheimer took

THE BLURRING OF TRUTH AND FICTION: LANCASTER AND SHELLEY WINTERS REUNITED IN THE ROLES OF FORMER SWEETHEARTS IN *THE YOUNG SAVAGES*.

over. Frankenheimer was familiar with the subject from his days at CBS, when a TV production about Stroud had been planned but abandoned owing to the uncompromising attitude of the Bureau of Prisons.

But, as Frankenheimer explained, 'In those days TV was done live, and I cannot to this day say what I was thinking of... because there is no way you can get birds to react the way we got them to behave in the film... Just to film the actions of one sparrow, we used about twenty-seven different sparrows. Thank God we were shooting in black and white or we would have had to paint the birds to look like one sparrow.'

Harold Hecht has said that 'Burt became obsessed by Stroud', and Burt himself claimed that he had 'never been so personally involved in a part before or since'. Indeed, such was his immersion in his task that when his beloved elder brother Jim, an assistant on the film, collapsed and died on set from a heart attack, he had the body taken away and continued the day's work, saving his grieving for his private time.

The shooting of *Birdman of Alcatraz* was a gruelling task. Frankenheimer had to fight for control despite having made it plain that he 'would only do the film if he [Burt] let the director be the one who made the final decisions'. The producers remained deaf to Frankenheimer's repeated warnings that the script was too long, with the result that the rough cut ran over four hours and the director was asked for cuts. 'You can't cut it,' Frankenheimer told them. 'It's a film called *Birdman of Alcatraz* and there are 120 pages of script before he even sees a bird, and that means 120 minutes of screen time. You can't cut it. You have to rewrite it.'

Lancaster had little choice but to agree to this astonishing circumstance whereby the film would virtually have to be remade. Frankenheimer went to work on the screenplay, and Burt joined an all-star cast in Stanley Kramer's monolithic, 189-minute courtroom examination of responsibility for the Holocaust, *Judgment at Nuremberg*. In a cast led by Spencer Tracy as the presiding judge and Maximilian Schell as the war criminals' defence lawyer, and including Marlene Dietrich, Richard Widmark, Montgomery Clift and Judy Garland, Burt had second billing.

The extroversion that had defined so much of his screen image now

ERNST JANNING BREAKS HIS SILENCE WITH A PASSIONATE OUTBURST. LANCASTER IN *JUDGMENT AT NUREMBERG*.

appeared to be on hold. The unsmiling DA of *The Young Savages* began what some critics have termed his 'repressed' period, well demonstrated in his performance as Ernst Janning, an internationally admired legal mind and former high court judge, on trial for perverting justice as the minister in charge under the Nazi regime. Unlike Paul Lukas in screenwriter Abby Mann's original television version, Burt was not ideally cast, and when the film was released several critics were eager to point out the disparity between the macho American and the ageing German intellectual. *Variety* said that 'Lancaster's role presents the actor with a taxing assignment in which he must overcome the discrepancy of his own virile identity with that of the character.' Others gave him full credit, with the *Sunday Telegraph* considering that he had 'a confessional outburst near the end which is easily the most striking thing this actor has ever done'.

Required to remain largely silent and grimly impassive throughout most of the proceedings, then to deliver a remarkable monologue

THE ANXIOUS PROSECUTOR (RICHARD WIDMARK, LEFT) AND AN IMPASSIVE JANNING LISTEN TO THE JUDGE IN THE NUREMBERG COURTROOM.

IN *BIRDMAN OF ALCATRAZ*
STROUD, NOW AN EXPERT
IN BIRD DISEASES, FINDS
HIS SOLITARY CONFINE-
MENT EASED BY THE
PRESENCE OF HIS EVER-
INCREASING COLONY OF
FEATHERED FRIENDS.
FILMING THE BIRDS WAS
A LENGTHY AND
PAINSTAKING BUSINESS.

running for more than eight minutes, Burt brought a brooding, domi-nating presence to the courtroom, together with dignity, palpable intel-ligence, and a stab at a German accent not much worse than the attempts of Judy Garland (a superb cameo) and Monty Clift.

During filming, Burt managed a quota of arguments, badly antagoniz-ing Maximilian Schell, but the film didn't suffer. Undeniably powerful, it grossed a lot of money, but caused controversy among those who felt that the subject of the Nazi atrocity should be laid to rest. This was especially true of the German press, who expressed their hostility at the huge première – provocatively held in West Berlin the day before Eichmann was due for sentencing in Israel. The cast defended the ven-ture to a man, but Lancaster at the last minute chose to absent himself from the première, claiming professional commitments to *Birdman of Alcatraz*. However, given his antagonism towards the press, it was widely believed that he preferred not to have to meet some three hundred of them from twenty-six countries.

In the autumn of 1961, with *Birdman of Alcatraz* finally completed, the actor took time out to relax, but his rest was cut short by the November brush-fire which broke out in the area, destroying over 400 houses, including the palatial Lancaster establishment. He evacuated himself and his family to the Beverly Hills Hotel, as did many others, leading the Associated Press report to remark that 'Most of those burned out checked into the Beverly Hills Hotel. It was probably the wealthiest group of refugees since the Bolsheviks drove the Czar and the Imperial household out of St Petersburg.'

He rebuilt the house on an even more opulent scale, with a $30,000 swimming pool that incorporated a waterfall.

Burt was philosophical. 'So many other people were affected by it that I couldn't feel particularly sorry for myself. It was just something that happened to all of us.' His phlegmatism was doubtless helped by the fact that $250,000 worth of paintings from his collection, which included works by Renoir, Utrillo, Vlaminck and Chagall, were out on loan to the Los Angeles County Art Museum. In due course he rebuilt the house on an even more opulent scale, with a $30,000 swimming pool that incorporated a waterfall.

Birdman of Alcatraz, the last film to be made by the Hecht-Lancaster partnership, weighed in at 147 minutes and opened in the summer of 1962. The director of prisons voiced objections to the film in a radio broadcast: 'I thought the glamorizing of a murderer like Stroud would

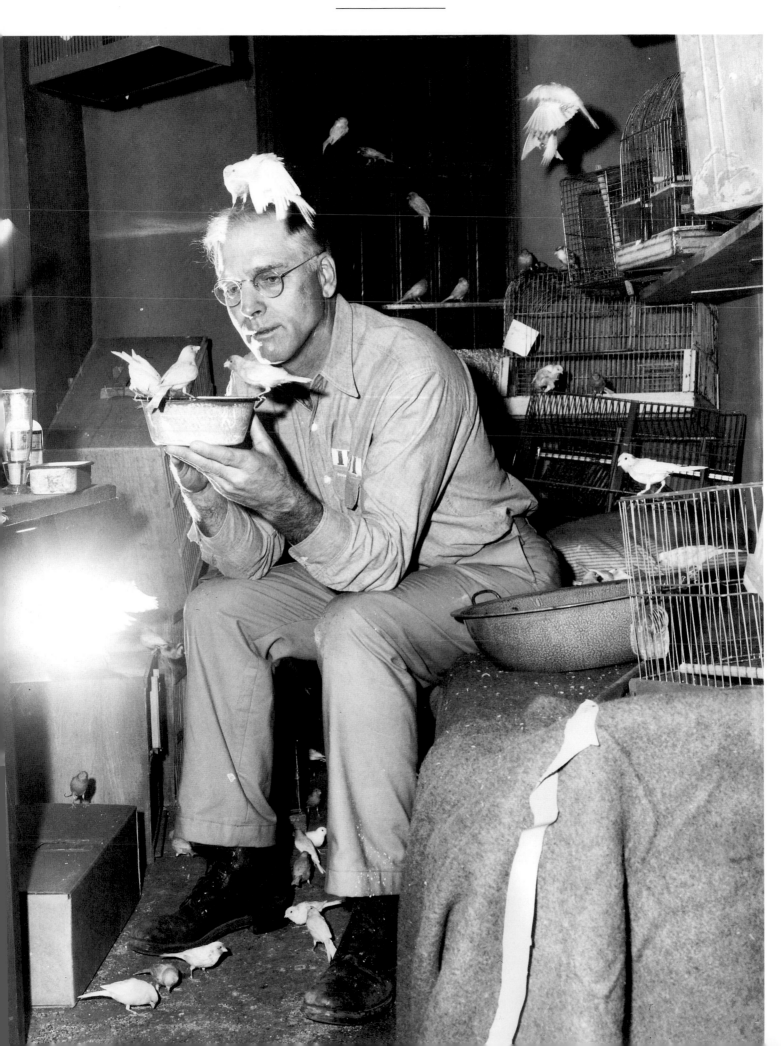

ABOVE: DISCUSSION OF A
KEY SCENE BETWEEN
DIRECTOR FRANKENHEIMER,
LANCASTER, AND THELMA
RITTER, STRONGLY CAST
AS STROUD'S MOTHER.
RIGHT: JOHN
FRANKENHEIMER LINING UP
A SHOT WITH BURT,
A PROGRESSIVELY AGEING
STROUD.

not be in the public interest and would be detrimental to our national well-being, harmful to our impressionable youth and a handicap to law enforcement.'

Burt issued a characteristically bullish statement in reply: 'Mr Bennett is not the censor of what the American people shall see, nor is he paid for this purpose. The public interest must not be confused with the hurt feelings of a group, nor does any such group represent the public. It is this "sacred cow" psychology which represents a real threat to the right of the public freedom of expression. The President's Committee on National Goals has drawn attention to the need for controversy, not for unanimity of expression.'

Lancaster was praised for 'notable realism, nuance and restraint' by the *New York Times*; the *New York Herald Tribune* considered that 'much of the suppressed power in the man and the film is due to Lancaster's performance', while *Variety* pronounced it 'the finest prison pic ever made'. Even the testy Stanley Kauffmann of *New Republic*, not a Lancaster fan, conceded that 'Burt Lancaster gives one of his few good performances'.

Critical acclaim was endorsed by a second Oscar nomination (Burt lost to Gregory Peck for *To Kill a Mockingbird*), and the best actor award at the Venice Film Festival. The film, one of Burt's self-confessed favourites, failed to perform as well as expected at the box office, but over the years has gathered a huge and admiring audience. Beautifully directed by Frankenheimer, and with first-class supporting performances, notably from Karl Malden as Stroud's reluctantly respectful nemesis, it remains absorbing and powerfully moving. Whether or not the real Stroud was as sympathetic a victim of circumstance as his screen counterpart is neither here nor there. In his portrayal, Lancaster deployed a combination of his best, as well as his most distinctive, qualities – brooding stillness, magnetic presence, suppressed rage, violent eruption and tenderness. The performance is restrained, subtly paced, and controlled by intelligence, sincerity and commitment, and the ageing of Stroud as the years crawl by is authentic.

In April 1962, a reluctant Burt was persuaded to appear on the Mike Wallace TV show, but stipulated that he would refuse to answer any

questions bearing on personal matters, including difficult professional relationships. Ignoring the stricture, Wallace questioned him about reported dissension on the set of *Judgment at Nuremberg* and raised the topic of Burt's explosive temper.

Burt attempted to skirt the issue, saying, 'There's no reason to talk about it. My temper belongs to me.' Wallace suggested that he was only trying to have an honest discussion; Lancaster replied, 'I am suggesting you are not. I think this line of questioning is unreasonable.' Wallace said that, as the talk show host, he had the advantage of putting whatever questions he chose. The now furious guest responded with 'I say you won't have the advantage long if we keep going like this', and walked out a few moments later. If Wallace's behaviour was crassly provocative, Lancaster's was unattractive, and it was fortunate for his public image that the show was not live.

A *Child Is Waiting* was irresistible to Lancaster, who had a genuine concern for the welfare of children.

Burt would soon leave for Italy to make the film generally considered the pinnacle of his career, but first there were two more commitments in the US. With Stanley Kramer producing for United Artists, a then newcomer named John Cassavetes directing, a script by Abby Mann, and Judy Garland co-starring, *A Child Is Waiting* was a labour of love that totally, and quite unjustly, flopped.

Kramer's taste for 'message' subjects was well known, and his new production was irresistible to Lancaster, who had a genuine concern for the welfare of children. Set in the Pacific State Hospital in Pomona, California, and, with the exception of the lead child (Bruce Ritchey), cast with the institution's actual inmates, *A Child Is Waiting* is a plea for understanding of retarded children, their families, and those who care for them.

Lancaster played the psychiatrist in charge of the hospital-cum-remedial school; Garland an inexperienced but dedicated newcomer to the staff who allows her personal emotions to cloud her judgement. She becomes particularly attached to one little boy (Ritchey), an autistic child abandoned by his parents – the child who is 'waiting' – and falls foul of Lancaster, whose objective methods she considers heartless.

The innovative Cassavetes brought a sharp, documentary quality to the proceedings, but there were disagreements with Kramer, who recut the director's version, increasing the sentimentality quotient. Garland, in one of her periodic emotional troughs, caused the on-set difficulties, while Burt, who liked her and was sensitive to her problems, was kind

and patient. The film attracted respectful critical reaction, but, although it is simultaneously thought-provoking and heart-wrenching, with amazing performances from the children and convincing work from Lancaster and Garland, audiences resolutely stayed away.

Next, Burt joined Tony Curtis, Robert Mitchum and Frank Sinatra for a cameo in *The List of Adrian Messenger*, produced by and starring his friend Kirk Douglas and directed by John Huston. In this witless, supposedly joky, farrago of a thriller, the guest stars were in disguise, and audiences were meant to amuse themselves by guessing who was what. All was revealed in a coy epilogue, and if Burt (in drag as a county Englishwoman vociferously protesting against blood sports) came off best, the less said about his participation, or indeed the film, the better.

Mountains of prose have been written about *The Leopard*, Luchino Visconti's epic realization of the highly regarded novel by Giuseppe di

BURT SEEMS BEMUSED, JUDY GARLAND APPEARS AMUSED, AS DIRECTOR JOHN CASSAVETES (RIGHT) DEMONSTRATES SOMETHING HE WANTS ON THE SET OF *A CHILD IS WAITING*. THIS WAS A RARE MOMENT OF LIGHT RELIEF IN THE MAKING OF A HARROWINGLY PAINFUL FILM.

LUCHINO VISCONTI

DIRECTS THE CARRIAGE

JOURNEY OF DON

FABRIZIO, THE PRINCE OF

SALINA, AND HIS WIFE

(RINA MORELLI) IN

THE LEOPARD.

Lampedusa. The account of Visconti's views, his almost neurotic perfectionism in reconstructing the period of the Risorgimento (1860–2), his working methods and his handling of actors and crew, is as fascinating as the film itself. The tale itself is especially well told in Laurence Schifano's biography of the great Italian director.

For Burt Lancaster, the unexpected challenge of finding himself at the centre of the film was a profound development in his life and career, which tapped all his resources, and led him into an attitude of near-subservience to the master in charge, whose autocracy exceeded his own.

The vast and costly apogee of Visconti's work, it soon became clear, could not be made without a substantial injection of American money, and producer Goffredo Lombardo reached an agreement with Twentieth Century-Fox. The chief role of Don Fabrizio, the Prince of Salina, was proving difficult to cast. Visconti was forced to abandon his first three choices: the great Russian Nikolai Cherkassov (too old); Laurence Olivier (unavailable); and Marlon Brando (Fox refused). The American studio offered the horrified director the choice of Spencer Tracy, Anthony Quinn or Lancaster, all unlikely candidates but, shown *Judgment at Nuremberg*, Visconti revised his opinion of Lancaster, the 'gangster cowboy'.

For the first time in his acting career, Burt found himself an outsider, marooned in an army of foreigners, including the aloof members of the Sicilian aristocracy commandeered by the director to play themselves. Initial resentment of this Hollywood intruder was palpable if unstated, and the intense and full-time application Burt put into studying Sicilian history and custom was regarded with smirking cynicism rather than admiration.

As Laurence Schifano puts it, 'Visconti received him suspiciously, quickly subjecting him to a reign of terror.'

In the course of the long shoot, during which Burt lived with his family aboard a yacht anchored off the island's coast, his colleagues came to realize the seriousness of his dedication. The barriers were dropped and he was admitted to the inner sanctum. His relationship with Visconti grew into a close one of mutual respect and affection, but not without the egocentric actor having to withstand being treated badly by the even more egocentric filmmaker. As Schifano puts it, 'Lancaster was a star at the peak of his fame then. Visconti received him suspiciously, quickly subjecting him to a reign of terror. Not only did he transform the American into a suave, elegant Leopard, but rendered him so docile that he became the director's admiring shadow.'

According to Burt's own recollections, 'When I arrived in Rome, I had a meeting for three hours with Visconti. He was quite surprised to find that I knew the book backwards, every nuance of it, and quite delighted to know that the people I'd lived with in my section of New York were Sicilians, and that I knew a great deal about the background of these people, and the Mafia and these kind of things.'

Visconti's delight didn't stop him from telling the actor that he had not wanted him for the role but, as Burt said, 'This man is a master. I rely on him a great deal, and he's taught me a lot about the Sicilian nobility. All right, he's a difficult man to work with, and I don't like being pushed around by anyone...

'Working on that film was a completely different experience for me. Visconti took endless pains to get everything right. He was a perfectionist. Yet he had this amazing way of trusting you. He wouldn't tell you how to play a scene. He'd let you do it your own way, once he saw you knew what you were doing. Once we did have a long talk – about three hours – on set about the approach to a scene. And the ideas he wanted me to get across were brilliant. They were far superior to anything I had in mind.'

Not only did Burt prove willing to bow gracefully to a superior mind and talent, but he learned to tolerate discomforts which must have seemed like humiliations in the context of his usual position. The indescribably opulent ball scene, which occupies most of the last third of the film, took forty-eight days of twelve-hour night shooting to complete, taxing the strength of the entire company to the limit. Much of the film was shot in the broiling summer heat and, with Visconti's methods, entailed an inordinate amount of waiting around. The director's adored favourite, Alain Delon, had the only dressing-room, and Burt was left to spend long hours standing in the dusty Sicilian fields. He also had to endure an outburst publicly directed at him by Visconti.

He felt it was all worth it, and the fate of *The Leopard* in the United States and Britain on its release in August 1963 came as a painful disappointment. The film

DON FABRIZIO ATTEMPTS TO INSTRUCT HIS WAYWARD NEPHEW, TANCREDI (ALAIN DELON), IN THE WAYS OF A CHANGING WORLD.

TWO GIANT EGOS, TWO DIFFERENT TRADITIONS, BUT VISCONTI AND LANCASTER, REHEARSING HERE, DISCOVERED MUTUAL ADMIRATION AND RESPECT.

was made in Italian, except for Burt, who spoke in English and was dubbed. Following the Italian preference, it was decided to dub rather than subtitle the film for the English-speaking market, and Lancaster volunteered his services to oversee the process in the United States. Despite his best efforts, the Americanization — of both language and accents — was a disaster, at odds with the period and subtle expression of the Italian original. Visconti was furious and distraught, but power-less to influence the studio executives, who virtually blamed Lancaster for the fiasco. To add insult to injury, the 205-minute film (already cut for Cannes to 185 minutes by the director) suffered the removal of another forty minutes. And as though this cruel and unbalancing ampu-tation were not enough, the studio reprocessed the print in bright, hard Technicolor, thus destroying the delicately glowing and painterly quality of the original.

In 1983, *The Leopard*, some of the cuts restored, was re-released in New York and London in its original version, with subtitles added, and

finally won the wider recognition it had been denied previously. In 1963, it won at Cannes and played to acclaim in Europe, but the massa-cred version was a box-office failure after most critics had dismissed it as a lumbering bore.

The assessment was not unjust. *The Leopard* is a complex tapestry about social upheaval against a background of revolution. Don Fabrizio, at the centre of events, symbolizes the passing of the old order. Recognizing the shape of things to come, he tries to provide for the future of his family by marrying off his nephew (Delon) to the wealthy daughter (Claudia Cardinale) of the new, equally corrupt, merchant class who preside in triumph over the death of the aristocracy while continuing to seek its favour. The film is a leisurely unravelling of events, at once sensuous, cynical and compassionate, with Lampedusa and Visconti's combined sophisticated social and political sensibilities (they were both born to the Italian nobility) as its controlling force. Like all great works of art, it could not withstand random acts of destruction.

Despite their lukewarm reception of the film, the American and English critics were generous in their praise of Lancaster. Britain's eminent Dilys Powell wrote that, 'Burt Lancaster as the prince is magnificent: each movement, each gesture has a noble authority, as if it were the product of centuries of ease, wealth and pride... The high impatience with the flutterings of his wife, the touch of arrogance towards the family priest, the ironic contempt for the new rich, the rage against a friend who cannot understand the impossibility of social survival without compromise, the sudden awareness of mortality: in everything his qualities persist.'

Granted Miss Powell had seen the original version, but if others who had not were less detailed and fulsome, they did not stint in acknowledging the depth and breadth of the actor's portrayal. Inarguably, *The Leopard* elevated Lancaster to a different professional plane, and remains an enduring testament to the capabilities that he frequently compromised.

'Burt Lancaster as the prince is magnificent: each movement, each gesture has a noble authority...'

The challenges and achievement of *The Leopard* failed to make any dent in his image back in Hollywood, where it was business as before — although his position on the Motion Picture Herald Poll, which charted the box-office popularity of the stars, had dropped to eighteen by 1963, and would continue to diminish as younger stars claimed pride of place. None the less, his clout in the industry was intact, and if the high point had been passed, there was still some solid commercial work and one interesting experiment to come during the decade.

He joined Kirk Douglas in the latter's production of *Seven Days in May*, his third outing with John Frankenheimer. Lancaster starred as General James Scott, the right-wing head of the US Joint Chiefs of Staff who is violently opposed to the plans of the pacifist president (Fredric March) to co-operate with the Russians in retrenching nuclear weapons. Scott constructs a secret underground base in the desert and masterminds a military coup to unseat the government, but the plan is discovered and exposed by his own aide, played by Douglas.

Splendidly cast and acted (with Ava Gardner in a telling supporting role as the general's discarded mistress), it was directed by Frankenheimer for maximum suspense, emerging as a superior conspiracy thriller with a powerful message. Burt, playing a character diametrically opposed to his own political affiliations, gave an imposing performance that critic Judith Crist remarked 'combines a finely controlled

RIGHT-WING FANATIC GENERAL JAMES SCOTT (LANCASTER) WITH COLONEL CASEY (KIRK DOUGLAS), THE TRUSTED AIDE WHO IS FORCED TO BETRAY HIM IN JOHN FRANKENHEIMER'S POLITICAL THRILLER *SEVEN DAYS IN MAY*.

IN *THE TRAIN*, DIRECTED
BY FRANKENHEIMER,
RESISTANCE LEADER BURT
MUST RELY ON THE HELP
OF A HOSTILE INNKEEPER
(JEANNE MOREAU) TO
CONCEAL HIM FROM THE
GERMAN SOLDIERS.

fanaticism with innate conviction', but the film, like many a similar politically liberal piece, was cold-shouldered, and it would be many a long year before Kirk and Burt joined forces again. There had been tensions on the set with, on this occasion, Douglas the thorn in Frankenheimer's side. Despite having asked his friend to star, the actor appeared to resent playing the secondary role. Frankenheimer was later quoted as saying, 'Kirk wanted to be Burt Lancaster — he's wanted to be Burt Lancaster all his life.'

Frankenheimer was back with Lancaster sooner than anticipated. Burt left for France to make *The Train* for United Artists, under the direction of Arthur Penn. Adapted from a book based on actual events, it was the story of Von Waldheim (Paul Scofield), an art-loving German officer who impounds the Impressionist collection from the Jeu de Paume shortly before the end of World War II. Lancaster played Labiche, a French railway official under the jurisdiction of the Nazi occupiers, who is charged with getting the priceless consignment to Germany by train. Labiche is a senior Resistance worker and, although he cares naught for the works of art, he is determined to save them for France. The film is no more than an actioner with some interesting overtones, and most of the 140 minutes of screen time is occupied with the efforts of Labiche and his cronies to sabotage the enterprise, and those of an increasingly suspicious Von Waldheim to push the train through before the imminent German defeat.

Disagreements and rows between Burt — who was involved as producer although Jules Bricken is credited — and Arthur Penn began instantly, and Penn was fired after a fortnight. Burt, as he had done with *Birdman*, sent an urgent SOS to a tired Frankenheimer, who unenthusiastically came to the rescue but once again insisted on reworking an unwieldy screenplay. It was a protracted shoot, dogged by serious technical mishaps and bad weather, and although the director brought his by now considerable expertise to making *The Train* as tense and exciting as possible, by the film's very nature (including an international cast with a conglomeration of accents), the result held no surprises.

Burt took advantage of weather delay in March of 1964 to fly to Washington DC for one day and take part in Martin Luther King's civil rights march, then resumed the work which, according to John Frankenheimer, he thoroughly enjoyed. 'He was in his element, falling from trains, sliding down ladders, climbing walls, yet all the time living his part.' (He may have lived the part, but he failed to convince as a Frenchman, not even attempting an accent – a decision he later regretted.) The show of physical prowess came from a man now past his fiftieth birthday, in great shape and looking good, but of whom Jeanne

THE BLACK-AND-WHITE FILM WAS MORE TENSE AND SOMBRE THAN THE BLOOD-AND-GUTS COLOUR PUBLICITY POSTER WOULD SUGGEST.

Moreau made an interesting, if waspish, comment: 'Before he can pick up an ashtray, he discusses his motivation for an hour or two. You want to say, "Just pick up the ashtray and shut up!" '

Next, reunited with director John Sturges, Burt made *The Hallelujah Trail*, a comedy Western designed for the newly modified Cinerama screen. He played US Cavalry Colonel Thadeus Gearhart, detailed to escort a wagon train of liquor to the parched citizens of a Denver mining town. Not only are Indians after the booty, but a band of Temperance ladies, led by the determined Cora Massingale (Lee Remick), travelling with them under Gearhart's protection, are out to thwart the enterprise.

The tale had the potential to charm and amuse – and occasionally succeeded – and its epic visual proportions allowed for much action, which it got. However, with the script growing increasingly confused, and the comedy degenerating into a mixture of spoof and wild farce, its 167 minutes grew interminable. Burt's decent comic stab at the harassed, mock-stern Gearhart couldn't rescue it.

Once again, filming was dogged by bad weather and, worse, the death of a stuntman who mistimed a cliff-top fall from a wagon. Critics were less than enthusiastic, and although the movie performed fairly well in special Cinerama showings, it was ignored on general release.

The star fared better with *The Professionals*, also in a Western mould, which reunited him with Richard Brooks and cast him, alongside Lee Marvin, Robert Ryan and Woody Strode, in the macho guise (an ironfisted, womanizing explosives expert) with which his American fans felt most comfortable. The simple plot has the four adventurers undertaking to rescue the beautiful wife of millionaire Ralph Bellamy, who has been kidnapped in revolutionary Mexico by one of Pancho Villa's toughest henchmen (Jack Palance). They succeed, only to discover that Bellamy is the villain, and the wife is with her chosen love, from whom he wrested her away. She was played by Burt's recent Italian co-star Claudia Cardinale, with whom he had forged a friendly and respectful

INTREPID TEMPERANCE CRUSADER CORA MASSINGALE (LEE REMICK) TRESPASSES ON COLONEL THADDEUS GEARHART'S TOILETTE IN *THE HALLELUJAH TRAIL*.

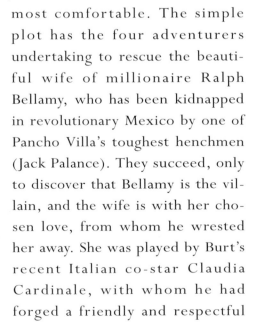

relationship and who, in a most uncharacteristic act, he invited to his home as a gesture of kindness to a foreign visitor.

Pauline Kael wrote in the *New Yorker* that *The Professionals* had 'the expertise of an old whore with practised hands and no thoughts of love'. Other notices were largely enthusiastic, with the *Saturday Review* considering Burt 'the most dynamic of the crew'. The film grossed almost $9 million in domestic rentals, making it one of the biggest hits of 1966 and winning Oscar nominations for Conrad Hall's photography and for Brooks' screenplay and direction.

It would be some while before Lancaster would again enjoy the sweet smell of success.

John Cheever's story *The Swimmer* is an allegorical tale about Ned Merrill, on the face of it a well-heeled Connecticut businessman with a wife and two daughters, who decides to swim home via a series of swimming pools in the neighbouring gardens of friends and acquaintances. When he completes the odyssey, which includes an emotional encounter with his ex-mistress and a series of increasingly weird and unpleasant incidents, he reaches his house only to find it locked and abandoned.

ABOVE: IN *THE*
PROFESSIONALS, THE
FIFTY-TWO-YEAR-OLD
LANCASTER'S STRENGTH
AND ATHLETICISM SEEMED
UNIMPAIRED BY THE ONSET
OF AGE.
LEFT: A ROGUE IN
CHAINS... BUT NOT FOR
LONG.

ABOVE: MEETING THE
CHALLENGE OF PLAYING
NED MERRILL, *THE
SWIMMER*, WITH COACH
BOB HORN.
RIGHT: BURT AND
SHELLEY WINTERS
ENJOYING THEMSELVES IN
MEXICO DURING A DAY
OFF FROM FILMING *THE
SCALPHUNTERS*.

That this offbeat and ambiguous story got made at all was a tribute to Burt's standing in Hollywood, though, in the event, Columbia Pictures, who financed the project for husband-and-wife team Frank and Eleanor Perry, took fright at the result and put the finished product on the shelf for two years, which is why no new Lancaster movie was seen in 1967.

Burt was sufficiently intrigued by the subject to overcome an almost hydrophobic resistance to water and go into swimmer's training. Clad throughout in bathing trunks, the fifty-three-year-old actor displayed a physique and an athleticism that were a remarkable testament to the fitness which he had religiously nurtured throughout his career, and his Merrill, full of bonhomie, bluster, confusion and vulnerability, is impressive.

However, the film poses more questions than it answers, and on its release in 1968, despite a degree of critical respect, it was an unqualified disaster at the box office. Burt, often an astute critic after the event, suggested that Cheever's imagination should have had a director of the ilk of Fellini to pull off *The Swimmer*, and his analysis of the film's shortcomings was accurate.

'It needed some kind of strange, weird approach to capture the audience and make them realize that, in a way, they were not looking at anything real. In talking about the script, we would say, "I don't know why two men in white coats don't come take this guy away." It should have been obvious that this man was going through something that was not quite real; it was all part of his imagination. But it was played in a realistic sense so, when you come to the end of that film, instead of being sympathetic and heartbroken for the man, you were surprised and shocked.' And, he could have added, thoroughly bewildered and frustrated.

Nowadays *The Swimmer* has found a large cult following and won Burt the admiration of a post-Lancaster generation. At the time, the most lasting significance of making the film pertained to his personal life. He and Norma continued to maintain the public face of a strong and happy marriage, but were privately miserable, biding their time for an

A DYNAMIC PAIRING:
OSSIE DAVIS AND BURT
AS UNLIKELY ALLIES IN
THE SCALPHUNTERS.

inevitable divorce. That time was now not far off and, on the set of *The Swimmer*, Burt met and fell in love with Jackie Bone, the unit hairdresser. The affair was conducted with discretion and remained secret until he finally parted from Norma.

Jackie rejoined Burt on location in Durango for *The Scalphunters*, a good-natured Western with a message of racial tolerance. Lancaster argued with director Sydney Pollack – who had impressed him during *The Young Savages* and had been called in at his suggestion to redirect a key sequence in *The Swimmer* – throughout the filming. Pollack refused to capitulate, thus earning Burt's highest respect.

The plot had loner fur trapper Burt teaming up with runaway slave Ossie Davis to recover pelts stolen by a crew of Indian-scalping bounty hunters, led by Telly Savalas. The white man-black man relationship lent the movie its special interest, and the comedy for which much of the tough action was played gave it appeal. Reviewers and audiences enjoyed it and it performed reasonably well for United Artists. Pauline Kael, who had described Lancaster and Davis as 'two dynamos', later wrote, 'There is so much talk now about the art of film that we may be in danger of forgetting that most of the movies we enjoy are not works of art. *The Scalphunters*, for example, was one of the few entertaining

ABOVE: AS MAJOR FALCONER IN SYDNEY POLLACK'S EERIE, AMBIGUOUS *CASTLE KEEP*. LEFT: A DRAMATIC DESCENT TO DEATH IN *THE GYPSY MOTHS*. THE TWO FILMS CLOSED THE DECADE ON A NOTE OF FAILURE.

FALCONER RIDES INTO TOWN, A KNIGHT ON A WHITE CHARGER. A SURREAL MOMENT FROM *CASTLE KEEP*, A FILM THAT, THOUGH CONFUSED, OFFERED SOME RICHLY IMAGINATIVE AND POWERFUL SEQUENCES.

movies this past year [1968], but skilful though it was, one could hardly call it a work of art.'

Shelley Winters — terrific as Savalas' seen-it-all, ex-whore mistress — and Burt were finally able to bury their past and enjoy working together. While in Durango, Burt took Spanish lessons and attended the Menotti Opera Festival. When shooting was complete, he and Jackie once more separated, continuing to meet secretly whenever possible.

Hollywood's most virile and athletic of leading men had begun the transition into middle-aged character actor.

The actor closed the decade with another film for Sydney Pollack and his fifth and last for John Frankenheimer, both released in the summer of 1969. Pollack and his star, fighting again to an alarming degree, made *Castle Keep* in Yugoslavia, where Columbia constructed an opulent castle (supposedly in Belgium), which a US Army contingent sets out to defend against the German invaders. The castle belongs to an impotent count (Jean-Pierre Aumont), posing as his beautiful wife's brother, so that she (Astrid Heeren) can lure a suitable man (in this case Lancaster, sporting an eye-patch) into her bed and produce an heir for the count's estate.

A curious blend of violence and philosophy, filmed in an almost surreal but shifting style, *Castle Keep* is a deeply flawed but very interesting film that was perhaps ahead of its time. Vincent Canby of the *New York Times* observed that it offered 'the form and beauty of a dark fairytale', and thought it 'accomplishes the dubious feat of being both anti and pro war at the same time'. Critics were otherwise divided, and though Burt was excellent, he failed to benefit from the ambitious venture, a box-office failure.

His last film of the year was also a failure. *The Gypsy Moths* was about a trio of barnstorming sky-divers (Lancaster, Gene Hackman and Scott Wilson) who arrive in a small town to put on a show and stay with Wilson's unhappily married aunt (Deborah Kerr). After much fencing, Burt and Deborah make love, and he asks her to go away with him. She refuses, and, preferring oblivion to the empty life he leads, Burt deliberately kills himself during the aerial display.

Hackman was superb, and Frankenheimer's handling of the daredevil stunts, the men and their machines swooping like great coloured birds, was breathtaking, but the plot and characterization were thin and fractured and the atmosphere bleak. Canby summed up *The Gypsy Moths* accurately: 'It's a weekend of dimly articulated emotional crisis for everyone, including Miss Kerr, an unhappy, highly unlikely Kansas housewife who has a brief affair with Lancaster, principally, you feel, because she remembers meeting him in *From Here to Eternity*.'

AS SKYDIVER MIKE RETTIG IN *THE GYPSY MOTHS*. THE MOVIE WAS AS DOOMED AS THE CHARACTER.

It was a disappointing conclusion to the Lancaster-Frankenheimer collaboration and to the decade which had seen the actor's most substantial accomplishments. Undoubtedly by the end of the 1960s, Hollywood's most virile and athletic of leading men had begun the transition into middle-aged character actor, and the next decade would see him in several roles which blended the attributes of the younger Lancaster with that of the man now approaching sixty.

In July 1969 the Lancaster marriage finally ended. Norma, by then aware of her husband's relationship with Jackie Bone, sued for divorce and was granted custody of their daughters (son William was now married) and alimony upwards of $2 million. As they had during their marriage, both Burt and Norma kept silent, refusing any public comment or discussion about their parting, and Burt started a new and happier life with Jackie Bone.

Staying in the game

The 1970s saw a sea-change in Burt Lancaster's life. The once golden boy, now matured into an often impressive character actor, could no longer guarantee marquee value on his name alone. He frequently expressed his intention to retire from acting in favour of production, but in truth he loved acting and never took the step. He did, though, maintain a production office for himself in Century City.

He had bought an apartment in LA, a beach house at Malibu and, his favourite retreat, a splendid apartment with furnishings and artworks to match in Rome. These homes he shared happily with Jackie, his constant companion. His divorce did not affect his relationship with his children (and grandchildren), to whom he remained devoted. His son William was the first to pursue a career in the film industry. He became a commercially successful screenwriter, beginning with *The Bad News Bears* in 1976. Later, Burt's daughter Joanna became a producer.

The decade saw dizzying contrasts of endeavour. In demand as a narrator of documentaries, he did this many times during the seventies, beginning with *King: A Filmed Record... Montgomery to Memphis*, about the revered civil rights leader. Other extracurricular activities saw him usher at a fund-raising event for presidential candidate George McGovern, and he made his first forays into the medium he had assiduously avoided, television. He appeared in an episode of *Sesame Street* in 1972 and, in 1974, on location in Italy with a stellar international cast, he played the title role in *Moses the Lawgiver*. (His son William appeared as the young Moses.) British producer Lew Grade's six-hour, $6-million epic was compressed and released in the UK theatrically – and disastrously – the following year.

Burt returned to the live theatre for the first time in nearly thirty years, realizing his wistful ambition to sing.

AS THE WEARY AND WORLDLY-WISE ARMY SCOUT MCINTOSH, IN ROBERT ALDRICH'S WESTERN *ULZANA'S RAID* (1972).

In 1971 Burt returned to the live theatre for the first time in nearly thirty years, realizing his wistful ambition to sing by appearing in a musical. This revival of Kurt Weill and Maxwell Anderson's *Knickerbocker Holiday* starred Burt as Peter Stuyvesant, seventeenth-century governor of New Amsterdam (later New York). The fans flocked to San Francisco's Curren Theater and Los Angeles' Dorothy Chandler Pavilion to see their screen idol dancing peg-legged (his own leg strapped out of sight) and hear him singing a score that included Weill's deathless 'September Song'.

'PEG-LEG PETE'! BURT'S RETURN TO THE LIVE THEATRE IN KURT WEILL'S MUSICAL *KNICKERBOCKER HOLIDAY*, STAGED IN LOS ANGELES.

Coached for the challenge by his friend Frank Sinatra, Burt proved to have a pleasing, if technically limited, baritone voice. The star and his audiences had a whale of a time, but critics were less enthusiastic. The *Los Angeles Times* commented, 'Oddly enough, his singing isn't at all bad. It's the acting side of the role that gives him trouble. To begin with, he is no more comfortable in period dress on the stage than he is on the screen. Secondly, he has to hop around on a silver peg leg that gives him too much to think about... It's an uphill fight all the way, and the applause at the end is more for effort than achievement.'

Lancaster himself cheerfully remarked that 'It was tough, all that singing and dancing up and down. I was marvellous but I got terrible notices.'

But what of Burt Lancaster, movie star? He is quoted as saying around this time that he couldn't afford to quit. 'Not because I haven't enough money but because, over the years, I've acquired too many people whose livelihood depends on my labours.' There was probably some truth in this, but the motives for carrying on were clearly, like the man himself, more complex. Whatever drove him, his filmography became something of a

As Mel Bakersfield, the stressed and harassed manager in *Airport*. An old-fashioned disaster movie which presented no challenge whatsoever to Burt, it grossed a fortune at the box office.

rag-bag. He was at his least convincing and most unattractive in roles which refused to bow to the changes which the passing of time had wrought, or playing cardboard characters which he seemed to treat with the contempt they deserved, walking through his performance with undisguised lack of interest.

His first release of the decade was *Airport*, the glossy movie adapted from Arthur Hailey's best-selling novel. Dean Martin piloted the plane with a deranged bomber on board, while Lancaster managed the snow-bound airport where Martin is trying to land. Directed by George Seaton, it was an out-and-out old-fashioned pot-boiler that moved critic Judith Crist to dub it 'the best film of 1944', but it grossed a fortune and spawned several sequels. Burt called the movie 'the biggest piece of junk ever made', but laughed all the way to the bank with the returns for his run-of-the-mill performance as the earnest authority figure, besieged by a collapsing marriage while trying to avert an air disaster.

After *Airport* came a trio of Westerns which form the body of Lancaster's best American work in the seventies, giving him the oppor-tunity to occupy legitimate leading man territory, albeit in character-

THE GRIZZLED, DIGNIFIED HERO OF *VALDEZ IS COMING*, THE FIRST OF THREE CONSECUTIVE WESTERNS AFTER *AIRPORT*.

actor mould. Edwin Sherin directed *Valdez Is Coming*, adapted by Roland Kibbee and David Rayfiel from an Elmore Leonard novel. Burt was Bob Valdez, an ageing Mexican and former US Cavalry scout, now a constable in a dusty border town where Tanner (Jon Cypher), a ruthless rancher, holds sway over the roughneck community.

In trying to save an innocent black man from being killed by Tanner in a mistaken act of revenge, Valdez is forced to pull the trigger himself in self-defence. The compassionate Mexican tries to raise money for the dead man's Indian widow, and the townsmen promise him a hundred dollars on condition that Tanner matches the sum. The balance of the

film is concerned with Valdez's determination to wrest the money from Tanner, whose initial response is to have him brutally beaten and strapped to a cross, leaving him to survive as best he can.

The film is a spare, character-driven Western with an anti-racist message, the violence effectively placed, and far superior to the negative criticism the subject and direction received on release in 1971. 'The film offers little besides its star,' commented *Time* magazine. The British press were more complimentary, and justly generous in praise of Lancaster. Dilys Powell found 'his portrait of Valdez, the humble slow-witted Mexican transformed into a figure of justice and vengeance, is

VALDEZ STRUGGLES TO FREE HIMSELF FROM THE CROSS TO WHICH HE HAS BEEN STRAPPED AFTER A BRUTAL BEATING.

persuasive as well as likeable'; but it was left to the *Sunday Telegraph* to define Lancaster's appeal: 'He belongs to a dying breed; a real star.'

Also released in 1971, *Lawman* was made by British producer-director Michael Winner with some expertise and, as might be expected from the man responsible for *Death Wish* and its sequels, was coldly and frequently violent. The lawman of the title is Jered Maddox, a US marshal with a fanatical commitment to observing the law, a distaste for unnecessary bloodshed and an obsessive horror of shooting a man in the back. Arrived in the town of

Reunited after nearly twenty years with Robert Aldrich, Burt completed his triple with *Ulzana's Raid*.

Sabbath to apprehend a band of killers, he finds himself up against a disillusioned marshal (Robert Ryan) who is in the pocket of a powerful rancher (Lee J. Cobb) and has abandoned any pretence of upholding law and order. The rancher's men are Maddox's quarry and, in waging a one-man battle against them, Maddox becomes a grim executioner, abandoning his principles one by one in the pursuit of justice.

LEFT: AS US MARSHAL
JERED MADDOX, THE
GRIM HARBINGER OF
JUSTICE IN *LAWMAN*.
ABOVE: IN DISCUSSION ON
THE SET WITH THE FILM'S
YOUNG BRITISH DIRECTOR,
MICHAEL WINNER.

A disturbingly ambiguous film, it was well summed up by Howard
Thompson of the *New York Times*. 'Some cutting dialogue and boiling
psychological tension are the most winning things about *Lawman*, a
potent but curiously exasperating Western,' he said, adding that there is
a 'baffling, oblique arrogance about the central character'. That Burt
imposed his presence on the film, a dark and troubled avenger, there
was no doubt.

Reunited after nearly twenty years with Robert Aldrich, Burt completed his triple with *Ulzana's Raid*, the most brutal and the most morally and intellectually interesting of the three. The story is essentially simple: a platoon of cavalrymen, commanded by an idealistic greenhorn
officer (Bruce Davison), is dispatched to track down Ulzana (Joaquin
Martinez), a renegade Apache who has escaped from a government

MADDOX'S OLD FLAME
(SHEREE NORTH) TRIES TO
PERSUADE HIM TO SPARE
HER HUSBAND FROM
PUNISHMENT.

reservation with a band of his men. The Indian leader is wreaking havoc on white settlements, pillaging and burning homesteads, raping and killing the occupants.

Lancaster played McIntosh, an ageing scout, cynical, detached and worldly-wise, who gently attempts to teach the young lieutenant lessons in reality. In one exchange, attempting to calm the fires of hatred and revulsion in the rookie, he says, 'Hating the Apaches would be like hating the desert because there ain't no water in it... You might as well hate the wind... Stop hating and start thinking.' And at another moment, when the issue of the white man's treatment of the Indians arises, 'What bothers you, Lieutenant, is that you don't like to think of white men behaving like Indians; it kind of confuses the issue.'

Aldrich intended the film to reflect the dilemmas and confused morality of the Vietnam War, then at its height, and his views were shared by Lancaster, whose liberal political stance was unwaveringly clear and consistent. The director made no concessions to delicacy in his graphic depiction of atrocities committed by Ulzana's men, and when the film was completed, Universal studios ran scared. They insisted on reshooting and re-editing certain scenes for American and British release (other territories got Aldrich's original version), thus weakening the film, which, to the bitter disappointment of star and director, failed to do well at the box office. Critic Vincent Canby recognized that 'The very ordinary plot does not do justice to the complexity of the film itself. *Ulzana's Raid* is a Western whose conventional outlines have been rather violently and beautifully bent by Mr Aldrich.'

Burt is on record as believing Alan Sharp's screenplay to be one of the very best he ever read, and his own performance was masterly and

McINTOSH'S LAST-DITCH STAND FOR SURVIVAL IN THE BLOODY AND COMPELLING *ULZANA'S RAID*.

effortless — a grizzled but strong figure, alert to the situation but resigned to its inevitabilities. As biographer Bruce Crowther puts it, 'He casts a powerful shadow over the film, even in the few moments when he is not on screen.'

It was released in 1972, the year that Lancaster, accompanied as always by Jackie, went to London to work again for Michael Winner. Burt rented a flat in Mayfair, from where he enjoyed the cultural riches of a city that he very much liked. He was often to be seen at Covent Garden, and discovered a new, never-to-be-realized ambition which he voiced to Roderick Mann of the *Sunday Express*. 'You know what I'd like to do? Direct opera. That's my great passion. I love it. Beverly Sills is a great friend of mine, and I'm always telling her I'd like to see opera singers trained as actors. As it is, they never seem to know how to behave on stage. I went to see *Otello* the other night and, really, it was on the verge of being ludicrous. I'd like to change all that.' He also enjoyed running in Hyde Park, and listening in at Speakers' Corner, and it was during this time that he gave his public interview at the National Film Theatre.

In working hours he was making *Scorpio*, an espionage thriller which teamed him with Alain Delon and Paul Scofield. The essence of the complicated plot had Burt as an ageing ('ageing' was the keyword for his characters during this period) CIA man suspected of being a double agent by his Washington boss. Delon is detailed to kill him and he tries to save himself with the help of Scofield, an old KGB friend.

Lancaster was excellent. His scenes with Scofield, which allowed both men opportunities to convey some depth of character, worked particularly well, and he proved himself still able to use his physical attributes as he ran through construction sites during a climactic chase on location in Vienna.

> **'You know what I'd like to do?**
> **Direct opera.... I'd like to see opera**
> **singers trained as actors.'**

CIA AND KGB ENJOY FRIENDSHIP IN ADVERSITY. LANCASTER AND PAUL SCOFIELD IN *SCORPIO*.

The wealthy and flamboyant Winner gave Lancaster the star treatment, calling him 'sir' and having his Rolls-Royce deliver elegant gourmet lunches from Wilton's restaurant to the English location sites. The object of this deferential attention was paid $750,000 plus a percentage for his labours.

However, the film was, in the main, critically derided. This was in part because the script was muddled and pretentious, in part because it seemed a lazy and derivative throwback to the espionage thrillers of earlier years, especially – with its zither music and Viennese sequences – *The Third Man*. As one critic remarked, only Orson Welles was missing from the brew.

Lancaster himself came out of it well enough, with his performance generally commended. One of the most interesting comments was made by Jay Cocks in *Time* magazine. 'Lancaster, always good at playing brashness, was never an actor to show much warmth. His role in *Scorpio*... gives him a chance to project the kind of dead-eyed savagery he has nearly patented as his own. He has the proper cunning and just the right kind of careful menace and restrained violence.' This is perhaps less an accurate assessment of Burt's performance in the movie than one man's view of the actor's personality and talent.

Burt was going through a period of delivering the goods in often respectable films, but to little avail. In *Scorpio* he has a line of dialogue which goes, 'The only rule is to stay in the game.' And stay in the game he did, albeit on occasion unwisely. After completing the work for Winner, he and Jackie visited Salzburg for more opera-going, then went on to Munich for the Olympic Games.

FILMING MEANS... WAITING. BURT ON LOCATION FOR MICHAEL WINNER'S *SCORPIO*.

169

Back in the United States, he accepted an offer from director David Miller, for which, because he believed the subject to be important, he accepted minimum Equity pay. *Executive Action* posits a theory about the Kennedy assassination in which a small right-wing group led by a businessman (Robert Ryan – a fine actor already terminally ill) set up Lee Harvey Oswald as a fall guy, while a crack team of their own hired guns, including an Oswald look-alike, carry out the shooting.

A discomforting mix of fact and fiction, filmed in black-and-white documentary style and intercutting actual footage of the Texas tragedy and its aftermath, it is a grim and strangely unappealing exercise. Released – somewhat erratically – late in 1973, *Executive Action* had a mixed critical reception, and caused some controversy. As an ex-CIA man in charge of training the operatives and organizing the assassination, Burt made little of a one-dimensional character. Pauline Kael aptly accused the film of 'matchlessly dull performances from a cast that includes Burt Lancaster (looking very depressed)'.

For *The Midnight Man*, Burt teamed up with his long-time friend and colleague, screenwriter Roland Kibbee. It was very much a joint venture, with Lancaster and Kibbee co-producing, co-writing and co-directing, but with Burt making the mistake he had once vowed never to make again — adding the lead role to his other duties.

The film was a convoluted thriller in which Lancaster portrayed a former policeman, jailed for murdering his wife's lover but now out on parole. Taking a job as a college campus security guard, he finds himself involved in solving a series of murders. With a poor screenplay and impenetrable plot, the film, which *Variety* predicted had 'a fair outlook in the popcorn trade', was a dismal failure. Kibbee gallantly shouldered the blame, saying that 'It was a concession to me because I wanted to make some money. It certainly wasn't the kind of project Burt would have picked out for himself... he has no taste for pulp fiction, and his reading is on a very high level...'

After this unsatisfactory period, it must have been some relief for Burt to return to his beloved Italy to make *Moses*, despite its gruelling thirty-two-week shoot and a lot of dissension. He remained in Italy to work once more for the now seriously ailing Visconti, who directed *Conversation Piece* (his last film) from a wheelchair.

The film concerned a lonely retired professor, living in lofty isolation with

his books and his art collection, whose privacy is invaded and equilibrium destroyed when, at the behest of a self-centred countess (Silvana Mangano), he lets out the top flat in his house to her son and his fiancée. There is an echo of Visconti's *Death in Venice* in Lancaster's growing devotion to Mangano's beautiful young lover (Helmut Berger), and shades of *The Leopard* in the dignity of the professor who must face change and impending death. Less happy reminders of *The Leopard* lay in the result of an international cast once again dubbed into less than appropriate English.

As *Moses the Lawgiver* in the multinational **TV** serial, later butchered for feature release.

A largely pretentious, overwrought and incoherent film, *Conversation Piece* was badly received, even in Italy, but Burt had some excellent reviews. Vincent Canby in the *New York Times* wrote of his 'formidably intelligent piece of work', and Britain's Nigel Andrews of the *Financial Times* thought that 'Lancaster alone lends the film some of the dignity and resonance it may once have had in Visconti's head. Rueful, aristocratic, stoically polite, his performance is a perfect companion piece to... Don Fabrizio in *The Leopard*.'

The actor followed this with a third Italian film, this time for the leading light of the new guard, Bernardo Bertolucci, capitalizing on the

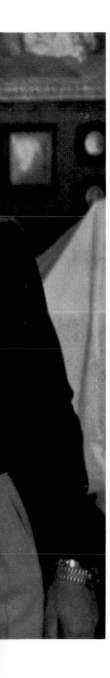

success of *Last Tango in Paris* to raise American money for *1900*. The finished film turned out to be a five-hour epic that had to be released in
two parts. It traces modern Italian history from 1901 to 1945, as lived
by the sons of, respectively, a wealthy landowner (Lancaster) and the
peasant foreman of his estate. A magnificent achievement, *1900*, owing
to its length, has never found widespread popularity. Burt's appearance
is relatively brief – he hangs himself in the barn during the first hour of
the story – but very impressive
and moving, and a far cry from the
material that came his way when
he returned to Hollywood.

Home again, he played the small
but effective part of Ned Buntline
in *Buffalo Bill and the Indians*, starring Paul Newman, for the brilliant maverick filmmaker Robert
Altman. Buntline was the dime
novelist who had mythologized
Buffalo Bill, and who, in Altman's
version, attempts to debunk the
legend he helped to create. The
movie was one of Altman's failures
and Burt didn't enjoy the assign-
ment because Altman 'didn't want to hear what your concept was, or
argue about it, and that makes work very difficult for me if I can't argue
with my director'.

As Ned Buntline in Robert Aldrich's *Buffalo Bill and the Indians*, Lancaster (left) took a back seat to a star of the next generation, Paul Newman (right).

By 1976 Lancaster's remarkable career appeared to be on a downward
slide. Joining Elizabeth Taylor and Anthony Hopkins among others, he
played Israeli Defence Minister Shimon Peres for the dreadful TV movie
Victory at Entebbe, topping that with his next feature, *The Cassandra
Crossing*. Reversing his previous indifference to financial considerations,
Burt admitted, 'There are times when I do a film like *The Cassandra
Crossing* simply because I need the money... It's a matter of lifestyle. I
have only one dress suit to my name, and a few jackets and pants but it
still costs me $300,000 just to live. I must continue to work.'

One assumes that the rest of the cast – Richard Harris, Sophia Loren,
Ava Gardner, Martin Sheen, Ingrid Thulin among them – had the same
problem. Directed by George Pan Cosmatos, the film's plot concerned
the havoc caused by a plague-infected terrorist aboard a train, and the
efforts of a high-ranking army intelligence officer (Lancaster) to deal

with the crisis. He does so by directing the train over a rickety bridge, thus killing the passengers. The script was risible, and Burt's role (and the playing of it) borders on a ludicrous parody of his better work. (Since 1994, the film offers the interest of seeing O.J. Simpson in a key supporting role.)

Released around the same time as *The Cassandra Crossing*, early in 1977, *Twilight's Last Gleaming* was a major film which should have been a success but wasn't. From the political thriller stable that spawned *Seven Days in May*, it has Lancaster as a renegade former military man, released from prison, who hijacks the Titan nuclear missile control station. He bargains with his old adversary, the military commander (Richard Widmark), and the incumbent US president (Charles Durning): either the president makes public the shameful truth about America's

ABOVE: CAUGHT IN THE WITLESS NONSENSE OF *THE CASSANDRA CROSSING* WITH INGRID THULIN, THE SWEDISH ACTRESS FROM THE INGMAR BERGMAN STABLE.

LEFT: THE MESSIANIC EX-GENERAL WHO THREATENS NUCLEAR DESTRUCTION IN *TWILIGHT'S LAST GLEAMING*.

participation in the Vietnam War by the release of secret documents, or he will release the warheads and blow the planet to smithereens.

Directed by Robert Aldrich, it is an often tense and sometimes interesting film, with a shocking climax, but is somewhat overlong and repetitive and the critics crucified it. Burt, masquerading as his former tough self, was uninteresting.

Despite the film's inadequate direction (by Don Taylor) and lacklustre production values, he was fascinating in *The Island of Dr Moreau*, a remake of 1932's *Island of Lost Souls*, which had starred Charles Laughton. Filmed in the Virgin Islands, the H.G. Wells story is about a deranged geneticist experimenting with turning animals into humans and vice versa, whose ghastly activities are uncovered by a sailor (Michael York) shipwrecked on Moreau's island. Although *Sight and Sound* preferred Laughton's 'manic zeal' to Lancaster's 'stolid mania', the latter role was intelligently conceived and all the more chilling for being played straight.

Lancaster reportedly sank some of his own money into *Go Tell the Spartans*, set in Vietnam in 1964, when America still had a relatively small number of troops there, ostensibly as military advisers. Ted Post's

THE ISLAND OF DR MOREAU: THE MAD GENETIC SCIENTIST WITH ONE OF HIS UNFORTUNATE ANIMALS.

LEFT: MAJOR ASA BARKER SURVEYS DISASTER IN THE UNDERRATED VIETNAM WAR FILM *GO TELL THE SPARTANS*. RIGHT: ENJOYING A BREAK IN THE SOUTH AFRICAN SUN WITH PETER O'TOOLE DURING THE MAKING OF *ZULU DAWN*.

film is gritty, realistic and interesting — an honest and unhysterical portrayal of events which deserved more attention and bigger audiences than it got — and Burt gave a rounded and impressive performance as a war-weary career major landed with difficult decisions and knuckle-headed superiors.

The decade limped to its undistinguished close. Burt went to South Africa to play an oddly accented English officer in *Zulu Dawn*, a prequel to the 1964 *Zulu*. He was given top billing in a glittering British cast, but the film made no impression at all. This was followed by *Cattle Annie and Little Britches*, his last, and least, Western. A raucous affair about two girls who hook up with a once legendary outlaw, it sank virtually without trace.

He left hospital visibly aged, his hair now white, and walking with some difficulty owing to an old knee injury.

Late in 1979 the sixty-six-year-old Lancaster became unwell. He was admitted to the Cedars-Sinai Hospital in January 1980, suffering severe abdominal pain, and was operated on to remove his gall bladder. Complications ensued during surgery and he was on the table for eleven hours. He left hospital visibly aged, his hair now white, and walking with some difficulty owing to an old knee injury which had caused him trouble over the years. But he emerged from his convalescence to give the performance that stands shoulder to shoulder with *The Leopard* as his most mature achievement.

Twilight's last
gleaming

In 1980, finally looking his age (sixty-seven), Burt Lancaster — although he had never really been away — made a comeback, starring in French director Louis Malle's *Atlantic City* and delivering a performance of finely judged perfection that many now consider to be his most fully realized achievement.

Lou (Lancaster), a former petty crook who dwells on memories of the big time that was never his, struggles to run his modest numbers game in a city now transformed into a legalized gambler's paradise. He is dependent for his living on an old-time mobster's hypochondriac widow (Kate Reid), whom he services in more ways than one. Lou courts a wistful involvement with a young waitress and would-be croupier (Susan Sarandon), which, for a short and precious time, offers promise when a stroke of accidental 'good fortune' brings him temporary riches and a sense of rejuvenation.

> **A performance of finely judged perfection that many now consider to be his most fully realized achievement.**

This elegy for a dead past, and mournful paean to a present peopled by losers, is beautifully scripted by playwright John Guare and directed with distinction by Malle, who drew superb performances from the entire cast. Burt none the less towers over the rest in a multifaceted, richly nuanced performance.

The reviews were uniformly enthusiastic, with *Time* magazine's Richard Schickel noting that 'The highest pleasure *Atlantic City* has to offer is a little essay on fastidiousness by Burt Lancaster. That is not a quality one automatically associates with a star who was once the most macho of leading men. But in the past decade, he has become a resourceful and wide-ranging character actor. Here he is playing Lou, who seems to feel neatness just might count in the battle to keep his

IMPECCABLY DRESSED TO KEEP UP APPEARANCES: SMALL-TIME NUMBERS RUNNER LOU IN *ATLANTIC CITY*, THE CROWNING GLORY OF AN EXTRAORDINARY CAREER.

ABOVE: LOU WAITS
ON HIS 'BENEFACTRESS'
(KATE REID), THE WIDOW
OF HIS FORMER PARTNER
IN PETTY CRIME.
RIGHT: UNOBSERVED BY
SALLY, THE OBJECT OF HIS
WISTFUL AFFECTIONS, HE
WATCHES HER IN HER
APARTMENT ACROSS
THE WAY.

withered dreams intact. You can practically smell the blue rinse in his hair; the pressing of a tie, the caressing of a whisky glass, the sniffing of a wine cork, incantatory gestures.'

Burt's efforts were rewarded with the best actor awards from the New York Film Critics, the Los Angeles Film Critics, the British Academy (BAFTA), and a fourth Oscar nomination. He lost out to another veteran, Henry Fonda, winning for the first time in his long career for *On Golden Pond*.

The 1980s, though they would offer nothing remotely comparable to *Atlantic City* in either scale or achievement, were a testament to Lancaster's durability and strength of purpose. His schedule of work was almost continuously full, and yet he found the time and energy to broadcast in a political protest against the Moral Majority, to campaign for ACLU, and to journey to Israel to address a gathering in honour of Kirk Douglas. There were several awards ceremonies to attend on his own account, and he served on the board of the Los Angeles Opera.

Meanwhile Burt's support of social causes remained unflagging. In 1984 he received the Mental Health Award from the University of

BURT LANCASTER WITH
DIRECTOR LOUIS MALLE
DURING THE FILMING OF
ATLANTIC CITY.

California for work he had done on a series of videos about the problems of mental illness; and in 1987 he was voted Man of the Year for his contribution to AIDS awareness in posing for a poster that was widely used in Los Angeles schools.

His personal life was not without difficulty. In the summer of 1983 he underwent a quadruple heart-bypass operation. His recovery was remarkably swift but, three years later, having asked him to co-star with Jane Fonda in *Old Gringo*, Columbia Pictures were refused insurance on the grounds of his medical history. The role went to Gregory Peck and Burt, showing the old fight, sued for $1.5 million. In 1985 his seventeen-year-long relationship with Jackie Bone suddenly ended. With his customary reticence intact, he never uttered a word on the subject and, like Norma before her, neither did Jackie. A year later, however, Burt found a new and lasting partner in Susan Scherer, exactly half his age. The couple married, in the presence of Burt's children and grandchildren, in September 1990.

Living and relaxing in his Rome apartment, where he grew his own herbs and cooked Italian food.

In August 1981 Burt had his final fling with live theatre, teaming up with Kirk Douglas for a production of the quaint and folksy *The Boys of Autumn* in San Francisco. It was autumnal indeed, with the two veterans ruefully admitting that they no longer had the stamina for repeated live performance, while none the less enjoying their roles as Tom Sawyer (Kirk) and Huckleberry Finn, reunited in old age.

The star's first film after *Atlantic City* took him back to Italy, where, setting the pattern for much of his remaining life, he made a little-seen film and appeared in a multi-million-dollar epic made for television. The film, *La Pelle* (*The Skin*), starring Marcello Mastroianni and Burt's old friend Claudia Cardinale, was directed by Liliana (*The Night Porter*) Cavani, and was barely heard of outside Europe, but he was well cast as Pope Gregory X in *Marco Polo*, the ten-hour TV serial. During this time he had the pleasure of living and relaxing in his Rome apartment, where he grew his own herbs and cooked Italian food, but he lost none of his capacity to travel elsewhere in Europe for purposes of work. He went to Germany in 1985 for *Sins of the Fathers*, a seven-hour mini-series made in English and tracing the fortunes of a German industrialist and his family across the two world wars. Julie Christie and Bruno Ganz were among the international cast headed by Lancaster. Again, this was not popular entertainment, but intelligent drama and, true to his lifelong pattern, Burt appeared in some less than edifying material during these years, of which *Voyage of Terror: The Achille Lauro Affair* was possibly the worst.

The actor added to his substantial body of work as a narrator of documentaries, and played host and narrator for TV's *The Life of Verdi*, in which Ronald Pickup played the composer. Numerous television films in the United States included *Scandal Sheet* (1985), which took him back to the territory occupied on a higher level by *Sweet Smell of Success*; while *Barnum* (1986), in which he was appropriately cast as the famous showman and circus owner, saw the actor, now seventy-four, back in the world of the Big Top.

In 1983, Burt enjoyed both the making and subsequent success of *Local Hero*, written and directed by Bill Forsyth and produced by David Puttnam towards the end of his troubled sojourn at Columbia Pictures. He played Felix Happer, an elderly oil billionaire and amateur astronomer whose eccentricity borders on nuttiness, a role that afforded him a long-desired opportunity, and one in which he was a thorough delight.

As the papal legate, later Pope Gregory X, in NBC's ten-hour mini-series *Marco Polo*.

Burt had loved the script, later remarking that 'It was light and satirical with no villains, just eccentrics. It was like those lovely old Ealing movies. I don't particularly care if I don't act any more unless I find a piece of work that really excites me.' The project almost foundered on the unaffordably high salary asked by Burt's agent, but when the actor heard about this, his response was, 'If these guys can't afford it, let it ride. I want to do it.'

On location in Scotland, he was kind and helpful, one of the company, putting up with problems and discomforts with uncharacteristic patience. Adored by all the cast and crew, the autocrat of yesteryear had mellowed. Soon after, he said, 'As you get older, you have to keep your mind open... I know now that it is not necessary to go through life

ABOVE: AS FELIX HAPPER
IN *LOCAL HERO*, REHEARS-
ING WITH DIRECTOR BILL
FORSYTH.
LEFT: ON LOCATION WITH
FORSYTH FOR *LOCAL
HERO*. PETER RIEGERT,
WHO PLAYED THE LEAD, IS
NEXT TO BURT, PETER
CAPALDI NEXT TO THE
CONTINUITY GIRL.

being a warrior.' He held Forsyth in high regard, and it was their mutual admiration that led to the two famous Foster's lager commercials that Burt made for Forsyth six years later.

His faith in *Local Hero*, a peculiarly British and small-scale film, was rewarded with appreciative notices. Vincent Canby in the *New York Times* thought Burt 'splendidly unpredictable as the oil tycoon. In Mr Lancaster's perfectly controlled nuttiness lies the secret of Mr Forsyth's comic method, which is as stylish and original as that of any new director to come along in years.' And Pauline Kael pronounced Burt 'Convincing as a man of authority whose only intimacy is with the stars above... he belongs there, on top of a tower under the stars, and I doubt if there are many actors who could convey so much by just standing there.'

Meanwhile the actor had played a CIA chief in *The Osterman Weekend*, an espionage drama that marked the return after an absence of several years of director Sam Peckinpah, but the film, re-edited by Twentieth Century-Fox, had little to recommend it. Recovered from his 1983 heart surgery, Burt went to Mexico to play Margot Kidder's long-lost father in *Little Treasure*, a small role in a slight, rather odd and forgettable film released in 1985, the year that he and Kirk Douglas joined forces for what can only be called a nostalgic nod in the direction of their shared past.

In theory, *Tough Guys* must have seemed like a terrific idea, reuniting two superstars in the twilight of their years, an entertaining acknowledgement of their status and their former glory. In practice, however, the script, written especially for them, must rank as one of the poorest that either actor had ever agreed to, and neither the direction nor production values succeeded in elevating it. The tale of two bank robbers, released from jail after thirty years to find themselves adrift in a totally altered world, had much potential, but in the event was a crude and vulgar comedy. It is a tribute to Lancaster's undiminished presence and his hard-won expertise that he managed to be quite touching.

He worked hard to publicize the film, swallowing his lifelong antipathy to press and TV interviews, and one can understand the sentiment that sucked both actors into the enterprise. But, as *Variety* all too aptly described it, 'Tough Guys is unalloyed hokum that proves a sad waste of talent on the parts of co-stars Burt Lancaster and Kirk Douglas. It's all silly, meaningless and vaguely depressing, since the awareness lingers throughout that both actors are capable of much, much more than is demanded of them here.'

Released in 1988, *Rocket Gibraltar* is a family story, best described as 'heartwarming', in which Burt starred as Levi Rockwell, the benevolent patriarch of a large family that gathers to celebrate his seventy-seventh birthday. Janet Maslin of the *New York Times* wrote, 'Burt Lancaster gives a wonderful performance... Wry and reflective, full of love for his family, but none too sugary, Levi is the pivot around whom the whole film revolves. Mr Lancaster is so touching that he makes it a disappointment every time the story wanders off elsewhere.' But *Rocket Gibraltar*, following the pattern of so many Lancaster films of the last years, was not very widely seen.

The same could not be said for his next, but the blockbusting success of *Field of Dreams*, released in 1989, heralded the arrival of a new heartthrob for a new generation, Kevin Costner. Burt's role was no more

BACK TO WHERE IT ALL BEGAN – THE CIRCUS. LANCASTER AS *BARNUM*, OF BARNUM AND BAILEY FAME, FOR **CBS TV** IN 1986.

than a significant cameo, playing a saintly old man who figures in Costner's strange odyssey but, as writer Angie Errigo put it, he contributed to 'the film's celebratory "old Hollywood" magic. It was a lovely swansong for a legend.'

LEFT: WITH KEVIN COSTNER IN PHIL ALDEN ROBINSON'S *FIELD OF DREAMS*, HIS LAST FEATURE FILM.

RIGHT: LOU AT HIS SHINING BEST IN *ATLANTIC CITY*.

Field of Dreams concluded the seventy-seven-feature-film career of the then seventy-six-year-old actor. In 1990, having made his Foster's commercials, he played the director of the Paris Opera House in a three-hour television version of *The Phantom of the Opera* for director Tony Richardson. After marrying Susan, his constant companion, in September, he left with his new bride for locations in South Carolina, where Burt began work on a new mini-series, *Separate but Equal*, with Sidney Poitier. He never finished the assignment.

On 1 December he suffered a massive stroke and was rushed into hospital. By Christmas he was home with Susan in their LA apartment, where, in time, he recovered a measure of speech, but was permanently paralysed down his right side. He remained in the apartment, cared for by his wife, frustrated by his enforced inactivity, but ever hopeful that he would recover fully. Visitors were few – mostly his children and Kirk Douglas – and the press were politely kept away. He was lost to the world, but not forgotten. In 1991, at a ceremony he was too ill to attend, he was awarded the Screen Actors Guild Life Achievement Award.

Obituaries were unanimous in mourning the loss of a unique contributor to film acting and filmmaking.

At the end of January 1994 Burt's lifelong friend and partner Nick Cravat died, after suffering from lung cancer. On 21 October the same year, three weeks before his eighty-first birthday, Burt Lancaster died peacefully at home.

Obituaries were unanimous in mourning the loss of a unique contributor to the profession of film acting and filmmaking. As Vincent Canby had once written in an otherwise unfavourable review, 'Mr Lancaster himself is simply beyond criticism, an enduring star whose screen personality – decent, liberal, tough, well-intentioned – provides the shape of the movies that are constructed around him.'

It seems, alas, safe to say we will not see his like again.

Filmography

feature films

1946 The Killers
1947 Brute Force
Variety Girl
Desert Fury
1948 I Walk Alone
All My Sons
Sorry, Wrong Number
Kiss the Blood Off My
Hands (UK: Blood on My
Hands)
1949 Criss Cross
Rope of Sand
1950 The Flame and the Arrow
Mister 880
1951 Vengeance Valley
Jim Thorpe – All-American
(UK: Man of Bronze)
Ten Tall Men
1952 The Crimson Pirate
Come Back, Little Sheba
1953 South Sea Woman
Three Sailors and a Girl
From Here to Eternity
1954 His Majesty O'Keefe
Apache
Vera Cruz
1955 The Kentuckian
The Rose Tattoo
1956 Trapeze
The Rainmaker
1957 Gunfight at the OK Corral
Sweet Smell of Success
1958 Run Silent, Run Deep
Separate Tables
1959 The Devil's Disciple
1960 The Unforgiven
Elmer Gantry
1961 The Young Savages
Judgment at Nuremberg
1962 Birdman of Alcatraz
1963 A Child Is Waiting
The List of Adrian Messenger
The Leopard (Il Gattopardo)

1964 Seven Days in May
The Train
1965 The Hallelujah Trail
1966 The Professionals
1968 The Scalphunters
The Swimmer
1969 Castle Keep
The Gypsy Moths
1970 Airport
1971 Valdez Is Coming
Lawman
Ulzana's Raid
1973 Scorpio
1974 Executive Action
The Midnight Man
1975 Conversation Piece
(Gruppo di Famiglia in
un Interno)
1976 1900 (Novecento)
Buffalo Bill and the Indians
Victory at Entebbe
(Theatrical release of
TV film)
Moses
(Edited version of
TV serial)
1977 The Cassandra Crossing
Twilight's Last Gleaming
The Island of Dr Moreau
1978 Go Tell the Spartans
1980 Zulu Dawn
Cattle Annie and
Little Britches
1981 Atlantic City
The Skin (La Pelle)
1983 Local Hero
The Osterman Weekend
1985 Little Treasure
1986 Tough Guys
1988 Rocket Gibraltar
1989 Field of Dreams
1990 The Jeweller's Shop
(La Boutique de l'Orfèvre)
(Made in 1987)

television films and series

1975 Moses the Lawgiver
1976 Victory at Entebbe
1982 Marco Polo
1985 Scandal Sheet
1986 On Wings of Eagles
Barnum
Sins of the Fathers
(UK: Fathers and Sons)
1987 Control
1989 Voyage of Terror:
The Achille Lauro Affair
I Promessi Sposi
(The Betrothed)
1990 The Phantom of the Opera
1991 Separate But Equal

live theatre

1945 A Sound of Hunting
1971 Knickerbocker Holiday
1981 The Boys of Autumn

Index